DYNAMIC TRADING INDICATORS

Founded in 1807, John Wiley & Sons is the oldest independent publishing company in the United States. With offices in North America, Europe, Australia, and Asia, Wiley is globally committed to developing and marketing print and electronic products and services for our customers' professional and personal knowledge and understanding.

The Wiley Trading series features books by traders who have survived the market's ever-changing temperament and have prospered—some by reinventing systems, others by getting back to basics. Whether for a novice trader, professional, or someone in-between, these books provide the advice and strategies needed to prosper today and well into the future.

For a list of available titles, please visit our web site at www.WileyFinance.com.

A Marketplace Book

DYNAMIC TRADING INDICATORS

Winning with Value Charts and Price Action Profile

MARK W. HELWEG
DAVID C. STENDAHL

JOHN WILEY & SONS, INC.

Published by John Wiley & Sons, Inc., New York.
Published simultaneously in Canada.

This publication is designed to provide accurate and authoritative information in regard to the subject matter covered. It is sold with the understanding that the publisher is not engaged in rendering legal, accounting, or other professional services. If legal advice or other expert assistance is required, the services of a competent professional person should be sought.

Designations used by companies to distinguish their products are often claimed as trademarks. In all instances where the author or publisher is aware of a claim, the product names appear in Initial Capital letters. Readers, however, should contact the appropriate companies for more complete information regarding trademarks and registration.

Value Charts and Price Action Profile are trademarks of Mark W. Helweg.

Wiley also publishes its books in a variety of electronic formats. Some content that appears in print may not be available in electronic books. For more information about Wiley products visit our Web site at www.wiley.com.

Library of Congress Cataloging-in-Publication Data:
Helweg, Mark.
    Dynamic trading indicators : winning with value charts and price
  action profile / Mark Helweg, David Stendahl.
       p.   cm. — (A marketplace book)
  "Published simultaneously in Canada."
  ISBN 0-471-21557-0 (cloth : alk. paper)
     1. Stocks—Charts, diagrams, etc.   2. Investment analysis.
  I. Stendahl, David. II. Title. III. Series.
HG4638 .H45   2002
332.63'2042—dc21   2002002970

Printed in the United States of America.

10 9 8 7 6 5 4 3 2 1

To Michelle, the most supportive and loving wife in the world. Also to my parents, who have always modeled excellence and who have always been an encouragement. Most importantly, I am forever grateful for John 3:16.
—M.W.H.

To the woman who has been there through it all and continues to be my support and the love of my life, my wife Carolyn. And to my beautiful daughter Ava, who brings me tremendous joy and happiness. Also to my parents and sister for their love and support. Thank you all.
—D.C.S.

Contents

INTRODUCTION

For all of those people who love trading or investing or simply want to gain more insight into market behavior, this book promises to offer two very powerful and exciting new tools that can be used to analyze and predict market behavior. To me, trading in the markets is like rafting through the gauntlet. The experience promises to offer a growing experience unmatched by just about anything else we encounter in daily living. To win as a trader, one has to control and even master different areas of his or her life. For example, you might be the greatest technical analyst in the world, but if you don't have discipline then you will probably never win over a long time period. You can't have intelligence and succeed without courage. You can't have discipline and succeed without a valid strategy. If becoming a great trader or investor didn't offer the challenge and growing experience that it does, then we most likely wouldn't be drawn to it.

Value Charts™ and Price Action Profile™ represent the most exciting breakthrough of my trading career. Consider the following definitions:

Price: The sum of money given for the sale of something
Value: An amount regarded as a fair equivalent for something

Price and value are two very different terms, yet we continue to look only at price charts. What we should be more concerned with is

1

the valuation of the market that we are studying instead of the price of the market. Price, as just stated, is the sum of money given for something. Value, on the other hand, deals with the issue of what price is considered fair. The meaning of the word *fair*, when it comes to the pricing of an object, might be defined as "a price level that the majority of both buyers and sellers deem as reasonable." After contemplating these definitions, it is logical to ask the following question: Are traditional price charts effective in identifying the valuation of a market? The answer to this question is no; traditional price charts are not effective in identifying the valuation of a market. This is logical because price charts accomplish just as their title implies; they display price. They were not designed to identify or define the valuation of a market.

Value Charts were developed to display the valuation of a market. When a market participant seeks to enter or exit a market, is he concerned with the price at which the market is trading or the valuation of the market? As we progress through this book, we discover that every market participant who enters or exits a market is really interested in the valuation of a market. The valuation of a market has to do with whether the current price level is trading at fair value, is trading above fair value (overvalued), or is trading below fair value (undervalued). The valuation of a market is determined by analyzing the percentage of buyers and sellers who consider current price levels acceptable, or fair. Value Charts were developed to define the valuation for any free market. Similar to normal price charts, Value Charts are most effective when applied to markets that are both standardized and liquid.

Value Charts were developed to pick up where traditional price charts leave off. Bar charts, as we know them, reveal only one aspect of price activity. More specifically, bar charts display the absolute current and historical price activity for a market. This information is beneficial if we are interested in learning about the magnitude of historical price moves. By reviewing this information, we can determine if a market is capable of experiencing explosive bull markets, able to sustain long trends, or simply prone to stagnant, choppy price activity. Traditional price charts remind us that big price moves can happen in certain markets over time. They remind market participants that significant profits can be generated by trading in these big price moves.

While traditional price charts express price in absolute terms, Value Charts display price activity in relative terms. Value Charts reveal the valuation of a market and define price levels in terms of being fair valued, overvalued, or undervalued price levels. By clearly defining a market's valuation, Value Charts allow traders to buy into markets at undervalued, or oversold, price levels. Also, Value Charts enable traders to avoid buying into markets at overvalued, or overbought, price levels. In addition, Value Charts allow traders to identify fair value price levels and confidently transact business at these price levels. Upon completing this book, traders will know how to read Value Charts and benefit from their ability to define the valuation of a market.

When you are contrasting Value Charts with traditional bar charts, it will become evident that each type of charting technique answers a different set of questions about the market under consideration. Many market participants have most likely never thought about the fact that traditional price charts alone may not be able to provide the necessary information to generate an optimal trading decision. Most investors have not asked themselves if traditional bar charts are an acceptable standalone primary source of market information for generating trading decisions. Whatever the case may be, it is important to understand that traditional price charts reveal only absolute market price behavior. Prudence demands that we take time to understand the effectiveness and limitations of the information provided by each market analysis tool that we are planning on using when making trading decisions.

When reading this book, you will learn that Value Charts work in tandem with another new and powerful market analysis tool, Price Action Profile. In order to determine the frequency that a market trades within each Value Chart price interval, it is necessary to study the corresponding Price Action Profile for the market under consideration. Just as the name indicates, a Price Action Profile plots the distribution of Value Chart price activity. As we will soon learn, Price Action Profiles allow investors to determine the degree in which a market is overvalued (overbought) or undervalued (oversold). By using conventions from modern statistics, this powerful complement to Value Charts enables investors to define Value Chart price ranges associated with fair value, overbought, and oversold price levels.

Value Charts and Price Action Profile were developed with both the novice and seasoned investor in mind. By simply viewing price in this new format, investors are able to gain valuable insight into the valuation of any market. These innovative new market analysis tools do not represent the black box. Rather, they represent a valuable and necessary market analysis tool that should be a part of every serious trader's arsenal of technical charting and market analysis tools. Value Charts and Price Action Profile meet the most important requirements of an effective market analysis tool; they are easy to learn, they can be deciphered quickly, and they can be interpreted only one way.

For trading system developers, Value Charts open up a whole new universe of relative price levels that can be utilized to drive trading systems and market indicators. Until now, most traders have had access to only a limited number of reference price levels. These price levels are used to instruct trading systems about when to enter or exit market positions. A *reference price level* is "a definable point at an identifiable time and price." Using daily bar charts as an example, the reference price levels include the opening price of the day, the closing price of the day, or the highs or lows of previous daily price bars. The high and low of the current price bar is for the most part undefinable until the trading session (day) is over. By utilizing Value Charts, traders can now create trading systems that have the ability to enter or exit markets at relative price levels intraday. The ability to define relative price levels, and hence relative value levels, during a trading period represents an exciting breakthrough in the field of trading system development.

Quantifiable information is useful information. Many market analysis strategies rely too heavily on the eye of the beholder when determining if certain rules or conditions are met. Market analysis strategies that rely on the judgment of a trader often contain too much gray area and have little long-term usefulness. Value Charts and Price Action Profile, on the other hand, generate quantifiable information that can be interpreted only one way. This allows traders to know when a certain condition is being met during the trading day, which allows them to act confidently.

Most importantly, Value Charts and Price Action Profile help keep the two emotions in check that have the potential to destroy the efforts of any trader, greed and fear. These new market analysis techniques allow traders to enforce discipline and avoid being suckered into the markets at short-term peaks and scared out of the markets at short-term bottoms. Pilots will be the first to testify that the artificial horizon is much more reliable than their physical sense of up and down. Without this key instrument, pilots would be forced to follow their own sense of direction and ultimately risk crashing into the earth when they exercise poor judgment. In the trading arena, Value Charts and Price Action Profile are the instruments that will help keep greed and fear in check for any trader. They have the ability to help keep traders who have typically followed their emotions in the decision making process from making costly decisions. The artificial horizon represents the current condition (orientation) of the airplane, and Value Charts and Price Action Profile represent the current condition (valuation) of the markets. Best of all, these innovative new market analysis tools were developed for anyone, regardless of trading experience, to learn and use. In writing this book, it was our top priority to keep things as simple as possible.

1

UNDERSTANDING PRICE AND VALUE

Price is defined by Webster's dictionary as "the sum of money expected or given for the sale of something." Using this definition, we can represent price by simply stating price in its absolute form, with respect to zero. This convention is used for almost every price chart used in the financial arena today. On the other hand, *value* is defined as "an amount regarded as a fair equivalent for something." How do we define *fair equivalent* when we are seeking to determine the value of something? To accomplish this, we need to solicit the opinions of the majority of market participants. For any given market they are the most qualified people to determine what price level is fair. It follows that a transaction in a market represents the vote from a corresponding buyer and seller on a price that both parties consider to be fair. It is therefore logical to conclude that many trades at a price level represent many votes for that price level representing fair value for the underlying stock, bond, currency, or futures contract.

The two requirements that are needed to accurately determine that valuation of any market are liquidity and standardized contracts. The valuation of a market can be established by referencing historical price activity, or past price levels where buyers and sellers have willingly met and transacted business. A thorough understanding of the current valuation of a market is very important when we are seeking to enter or exit market positions. The experience of buying a used car serves as an excellent example of how historical price data are used to understand the current market valuation. Unlike the new car market, where price fixing by the manufacturers impacts the market price, the used car market is solely influenced by supply and demand forces.

THE CAR BUYING PROCESS

At some point in most of our lives we are all forced to purchase a used automobile. This process usually involves identifying the automobiles that meet our general requirements and then narrowing our choices down to the one particular make and model that most effectively meets our needs. For this example, we will assume that we are interested in purchasing a used vehicle because the used car market more accurately represents a free market environment when compared to the new car market. Once we are able to identify the make and model of the used vehicle that we are interested in buying, we will start to shop around for this particular automobile.

As we begin to shop for this automobile, we need to somehow have the ability to define the fair value price level for the vehicle that we are interested in purchasing. Once we have identified the price level that list fair value, we can then start to hunt for the best deal. Ordinarily, we will reference the Blue Book, which ideally should list the price level that the mass market considers to be acceptable by both buyers and sellers, or the fair value price level. In other words, this fair value price level is the price level at which the majority of buyers and sellers have agreed to transact business. Ideally, if we were to take all the recent transactional price data from the used car market for the make and model that we are interested in buying, we should be able to average these numbers and come up with the same fair value price listed in the Blue Book. The Blue Book price should represent the fair value price.

We need the Blue Book fair value price so that we can have a reference price level to compare the asking prices quoted to us by the sellers of the vehicles under consideration. In this example, we will assume that our used car market is a standardized market because we can make adjustments to the asking price for things like excessive mileage or upgraded features. Upon referencing the Blue Book, we will assume that the fair value asking price for the year, make, and model car that we are looking to purchase is $10,000. After referencing the Internet and the local newspaper, we will assume that we are able to locate 15 like automobiles for sale and record their asking prices (see Table 1.1). For practical purposes, we will assume that all the automobiles have exactly the same color, are the same year, make, and model, and have the same mileage. By making this assumption, we will satisfy the requirement of having a standardized market. Therefore, the prices listed in Table 1.1 will represent prices for 15 vehicles that are functionally and cosmetically identical.

All things being equal, it looks as though our efforts have paid off in one respect. By reviewing Table 1.1, we can clearly see that there are sellers who are willing to sell their used cars for less than the Blue Book fair value price of $10,000. The prices significantly lower than the fair value price of $10,000 represent undervalued price quotes and better deals for the buyer. The asking prices significantly above the $10,000 fair value price level represent overvalued price quotes and unattractive deals for the buyer. We can present the price data in Table 1.1 in a histogram chart in order to reveal information in a more useful format as seen in Figure 1.1.

As you can see, the histogram in Figure 1.1 displays the asking prices from the data in Table 1.1. This histogram somewhat resembles a crude bell curve. The majority of asking prices occurred within plus or minus $500 from the Blue Book fair value price of

Table 1.1 Individual asking prices listed by sellers of a specific make, model, and year automobile

Seller 1	$10,800	Seller 6	$ 9,400	Seller 11	$ 8,800
Seller 2	$ 9,900	Seller 7	$ 9,900	Seller 12	$10,250
Seller 3	$ 9,250	Seller 8	$11,400	Seller 13	$10,750
Seller 4	$ 9,700	Seller 9	$10,100	Seller 14	$10,499
Seller 5	$11,999	Seller 10	$ 9,950	Seller 15	$10,300

Figure 1.1   Histogram of asking prices from Table 1.1

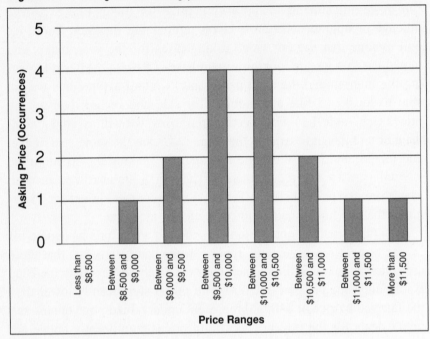

$10,000. We would expect that the majority of asking prices would be fairly close to the Blue Book fair value price of $10,000 if the Blue Book price did indeed represent fair value. The fair value price should approximately equal the average of the recent prices recorded from actual transactions for the automobiles that we are considering.

Additional analysis of Figure 1.1 reveals that there are several asking prices located further away from the $10,000 fair value price level. We can see that there are a total of three asking prices less than $9,500 and a total of four asking prices that are greater than $10,500. Clearly, if the automobiles listed for sale in Table 1.1 have been normalized and represent the same vehicles or the same product, the asking price of $8,800 offered by Seller 11 represents the best deal. Although the histogram displayed in Figure 1.1 allows us to visually determine the attractiveness of each of the asking prices in Table 1.1, we can present this information in an even more effective format (see Figure 1.2). Figure 1.2 is easier to analyze because the price axis is positioned along the *y*-axis, or vertical axis. This format is the most accepted convention for displaying price charts.

Figure 1.2 displays the price datum listed in Table 1.1 in a slightly different format when compared to Figure 1.1. By organiz-

Figure 1.2 Frequency histogram of sales prices from Table 1.1

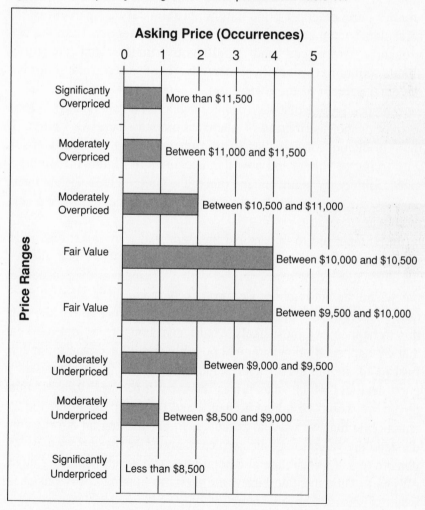

ing the sales prices into a basic histogram, we are able to easily see if a specific asking price is fair, overpriced, or underpriced. The categories used to label the frequency histogram bars in Figure 1.2 are not arbitrary. As we will learn in the upcoming chapters, we can organize price data into different valuation categories by utilizing statistical conventions. For example, the category defined as fair value should contain the majority of the price data (approximately 68 percent of the price data). The moderately overpriced and the moderately underpriced categories should contain a smaller percentage of price data (approximately 27 percent of the price data) when compared to the fair value category. Last, the significantly overpriced and significantly underpriced categories should contain the smallest percentage of price data (approximately 5 percent of the price data).

The percentage that each category should contain is derived from a study of the distribution of a normal mound-shaped bell curve. If the introduction of statistics is intimidating, don't concern yourself with trying to understand how the categories in Figure 1.2 are organized. Simply try to understand that the asking prices associated with each category represent a more or less attractive deal to us, the potential buyer.

It is important to understand the steps that were taken that allow us to identify the most undervalued automobile. If we had allowed ourselves to become overwhelmed with excitement at the prospect of purchasing an automobile, we most likely would have allowed emotions to negatively impact our decision-making process. By allowing this to happen, we most likely would have bought the first used car that we happened upon and quite possibly could have paid too much. Instead of attempting to understand which sales prices represent a good deal and which sales prices represent a bad deal to a potential buyer, we would be taking a chance and potentially overpay for the automobile that we want to purchase. In not making an effort to understand the valuation of the used car market, we make ourselves vulnerable to sellers who are attempting to catch an unsuspecting buyer off guard. Unsuspecting buyers are prone to making costly mistakes, whereas educated buyers are not.

UNDERSTANDING THE CAR BUYING PROCESS

It is important to understand several key points in the previous example. First of all, the general trend of the used car market was not taken into consideration. Figure 1.2 helped us, the buyer, to identify an attractive market entry price. The strategy of entering a market at an optimal price level is a different issue from determining the long-term trend of the market. However, it is just as important to overall investing as putting is to the game of golf. It was once said about the game of golf that "you drive for show and put for dough." In other words, the big success will come when you master the short game. The same principle holds true for trading. Determining the optimal entry and exit points, the short game in the market is every bit as important as determining the long-term trend.

Some readers may think that the car-buying example illustrates common sense put to work. If you fall into this camp, then it would be worthwhile to consider the following observation. Suppose that the histogram chart in Figure 1.2 was made available to you before you started to price shop for your used automobile. A wealth of information is revealed by the histogram in Figure 1.2. We would have had a firm understanding of the market before we had even begun to price shop. First, we would have known what price levels were high or unreasonable, what price levels were fair, and what price levels were attractive to buyers. As we reviewed the different asking prices listed in the newspaper, we would have immediately known if the asking price was reasonable. If we had stumbled upon a seller who wasn't in tune with the market and was selling his vehicle for much less than it was worth, we would have been in a position to immediately act upon the opportunity with confidence. It is important to understand that great deals do not last long. The ability to recognize and define a great deal or an undervalued asset is extremely valuable. The chart in Figure 1.2 clearly defines what price levels constitute a great deal and allows buyers to act immediately when confronted with an attractive opportunity.

If we needed to purchase an automobile in a fairly short amount of time, we should be able to identify several asking prices in the fair value price range. Most importantly, we could avoid paying too much by identifying price levels that constituted moderately overpriced and significantly overpriced levels. A buyer who is caught off guard and buys an overpriced vehicle will have difficulty recouping his investment in the event that he has to turn around and sell the vehicle in the near future. He would most likely be forced to take a loss because he had paid too much for the vehicle in the first place.

THE TYPICAL INVESTING PROCESS

The process of entering the stock market is much the same as the process of entering the used car market. However, most investors are completely missing a short game when it comes to buying and selling stocks, for example. There is no such thing as a good golfer who completely ignores his or her short game. All the great golfers will testify that their short games can make or break their overall performances.

Incredibly, most investors spend more time price shopping for a washer and dryer than they do determining the optimal entry point for a stock purchase. While investors may save $50 on the purchase of a new washer and dryer by understanding and identifying a good deal, they arbitrarily enter and exit the stock market where significantly more money is at stake. The primary reason why investors do not spend time finding the best deal when they are entering and exiting the stock market is because they do not have the tools necessary to define what is meant by a good deal. Investors need a Blue Book equivalent for the stock market to help them understand fair value. So Value Charts were developed to be the Blue Book for the stock, bond, currency, and futures markets.

The typical investing process usually involves taking time to select what stock to buy. Investors often spend considerable time analyzing fundamental information, including annual reports and PE ratios, when determining what stocks to purchase. Once this process is completed and a stock is selected, the average investor arbitrarily enters the market. These same investors would most likely never go out and arbitrarily buy the first car that they find for sale after determining the make and model that they wanted. Yet most market participants arbitrarily enter and exit their market positions.

In order to offer a solution that enables investors to enter and exit the markets at attractive price levels, it is necessary to understand the tools that are currently available in the investment arena. Just as newspapers serve to provide price data for car buyers in the used car markets, exchanges from all over the world report price information that is ultimately utilized to construct price charts. These price (bar) charts in turn communicate information to investors about stock markets, bond markets, currency markets, and futures markets. Unfortunately, until now there has been no equivalent to the Blue Book used in the automotive industry available to investors in the financial world. Furthermore, there is presently no charting tool (histogram), similar to the one found in Figure 1.2, available for investors to understand and define the valuation of a market. In order to improve the investment process and allow investors to strategically enter and exit the markets, we need to understand the strengths and weaknesses of traditional charting tools.

THE LIMITATIONS OF TRADITIONAL PRICE CHARTS

As we seek to understand the difference between price and value, it is important to note that value is a function of time whereas price is not a function of time. Price is absolute and is unaffected by the passing of time. A price quote to sell IBM stock, for example, may be underpriced (undervalued in the minds of most market participants) and a great buy today whereas six months from today, the same price quote may be overpriced (overvalued in the minds of most market participants) and hence a poor buy.

Most traders utilize some form of price charts to analyze markets. The most common form of traditional price charts is the bar chart, which displays the open, high, low, and close of a market (as seen in Figure 1.3).

Price activity from General Electric stock is displayed in Figure 1.3. This chart serves as a good example of a traditional bar chart. As we all know, each price bar is plotted with respect to zero. Zero serves

Figure 1.3   Daily bar chart of General Electric stock prices

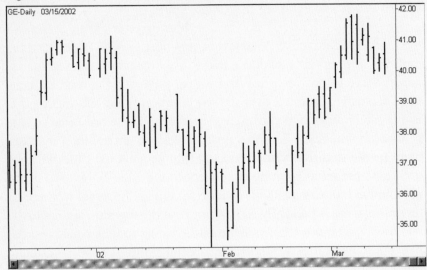

Chart created with TradeStation® 2000i by Omega Research, Inc.

as the reference point for every traditional price chart. For example, General Electric closed at $40.19 on March 15, 2002. The closing price of $40.19 represents $40.19 above zero. These charts are valuable for displaying the magnitude of both the current and the historical price movements of a market. We can clearly see by viewing this chart that General Electric moved from $36.84 to $40.19 in Figure 1.3 and that it is trading within a range. By viewing traditional price charts, we can determine if a market is experiencing a significant price move and trending, is choppy and range bound, or is simply stagnant.

Traditional price charts, however, are not effective in revealing the valuation of a market. They are not useful for identifying relative overbought and oversold price levels. Traditional price charts are not able to identify and define undervalued price levels, overvalued price levels, or prices associated with fair value. In hindsight, we can identify overbought and oversold price levels, but they are not easily detectable in real-time trading. It is possible to observe that a market has sold off from recent highs or rallied from recent lows, but it is difficult to quantify the exact valuation of the current price level when we are

using traditional price charts. Because the goal of every market participant is to buy into underpriced (undervalued) markets and sell into
overpriced (overvalued) markets, we need to have the ability to chart
price in such a way as to allow a trader to define underpriced or overpriced price levels. Take a minute to study the bar chart containing
four price bars in Figure 1.4.

After viewing the four daily price bars in Figure 1.4, answer the
following question. Which statement accurately describes the last
three daily price bars B, C, and D?

1. The last three daily price bars are identical and represent the same
   value because they have the same opening, high, low, and closing
   prices.
2. The last three price bars represent different values even though
   they have the same opening, high, low, and closing prices.

The correct answer is 2, the last three price bars represent different
values even though they have the same opening, high, low, and closing prices. At first this statement may not make a lot of sense. When
we really stop and analyze the last three price bars we will see that
they are different because each price bar represents a different day

Figure 1.4   Four daily price bars

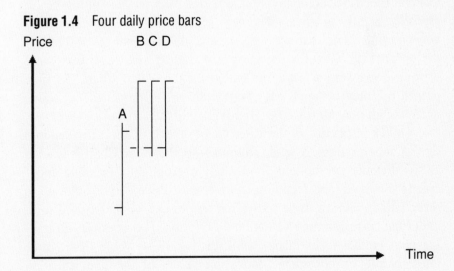

(time period). When the last three days are analyzed in terms of value, day C represents a different value from day B and day D represents a different value from days B and C. At the close of day B the market seems to be somewhat overbought when compared to day A. Day C seems to be somewhat less overbought than day B because the market has traded at that price level for two days. Last, day D seems to be less overbought and closer to fair value than days B and C because the market has now traded in this price range for three days and buyers and sellers appear to be comfortable transacting business at these price levels.

Although traditional bar charts present the last three bars displayed in Figure 1.4 as though they were identical, they are different when we are considering the valuation of the price levels during each day. The valuation of a market is determined by comparing current prices to the price history of that market. As time passes, price history becomes less relevant in determining market valuation. Trading activity that took place yesterday will be considered much more relevant to the short-term valuation of a market than would trading activity that took place last year.

We can now view both the traditional bar chart for General Electric (as displayed in Figure 1.3) and the corresponding Value Chart for General Electric accompanying it. The first 10 price bars in Figure 1.5 represent a rally in prices. The next eight price bars represent sideways trading. Note that although these eight price bars (identified by the up arrows) were for the most part trading sideways, they were drifting downward toward fair value on the Value Chart. As time passed by, they became less overbought and approached fair value even though they all traded at approximately the same price level.

A quick inspection of the Value Chart reveals that it is divided into five valuation ranges. Starting from the top, the Value Chart is labeled as significantly overbought, moderately overbought, fair value, moderately oversold, and significantly oversold. Price activity that takes place within each of these individual ranges can be understood to fit under the corresponding valuation description. For example, all trading activity that takes place within the –4 to +4 Value Chart price range would be considered fair value. Each of the five valuation

Figure 1.5   Daily Value Chart of General Electric stock prices

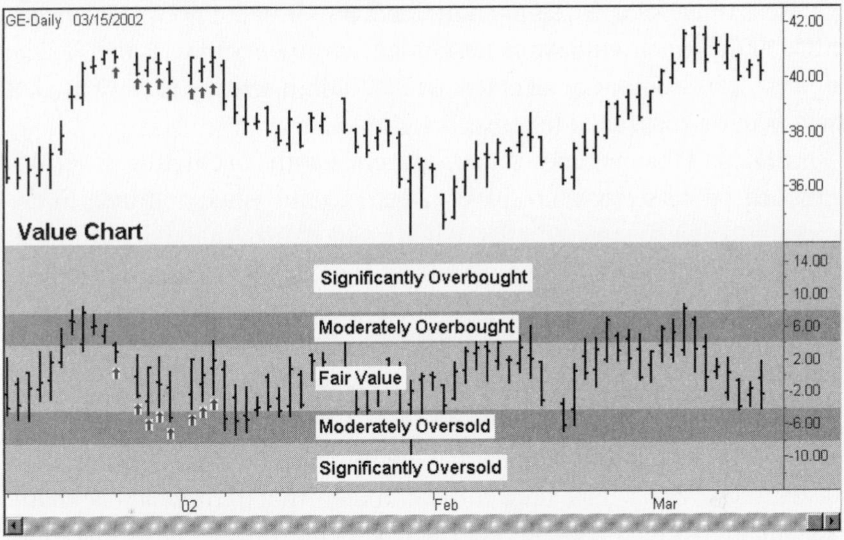

Chart created with TradeStation® 2000i by Omega Research, Inc.

ranges can be distinguished by their different shades, as seen in Figure 1.5. The Value Chart price levels that separate the different valuation ranges will be covered in much greater detail in Chapter 2.

FAIR VALUE

The valuation of a market is a function of both price and time. If a free market traded at the same price forever, one would logically assume that the buyers and sellers agreed that the price is not overbought or oversold, but representative of fair value. The markets that we participate in are rarely trading at the exact same price over time, but instead are constantly overshooting fair value, both to the upside and the downside, across every time frame. Because we live in an ever changing world, fair value is constantly being redefined as time goes on. Actively traded markets are always oscillating around fair value.

The market is made up of many individual participants who are in a constant search for fair value across every time frame. We primarily concern ourselves with the analysis of short-term market valuation when using Value Charts and Price Action Profile in this book. Regardless of an investor's time horizon, every investor needs to concern himself or herself with short-term price activity in order to identify the optimal entry or exit point. Most of the trading activity for any market will occur around the fair value price level.

Prices, as previously stated, are constantly oscillating from degrees of being overbought (overvalued) to fair value and then to degrees of being oversold (undervalued), and so on. Although traditional bar charts are useful when we are analyzing historical price movement, they are not an effective tool for identifying fair value, relative overbought, or relative oversold price levels. As we previously note, two identical price bars on a traditional bar chart are not necessarily equal in terms of value. Knowing this we need a price chart that can identify relative overbought price levels, relative oversold price levels, and fair value. This need to accomplish what traditional bar charts are unable to accomplish is what led to the development of Value Charts, which is discussed in Chapter 2. Before we begin learning about Value Charts, we need to appreciate the key elements of an effective market analysis tool.

ASPECTS OF AN EFFECTIVE MARKET ANALYSIS TOOL

There are several important requirements that an effective market analysis tool should possess. First of all, because opportunity is a function of time, effective market analysis techniques must condense information. It was once said that a picture is worth a thousand words. A picture can be interpreted much quicker than a written document that describes the same subject. Consider the following example.

We start by viewing the price activity from General Motors stock. As you can see in Figure 1.6, the least efficient way in which to present the price activity of a market is in plain text. How long would it take us to effectively analyze these price data? We would most likely need to invest a considerable amount of time to create a mental image of what the price of General Motors did during this time period. Clearly, if we had to rely on price data displayed in a text format to analyze markets, we would be limited to analyzing a small group of markets because of time constraints. Furthermore, we would have to expend a lot of energy to create a mental picture of what actually took place in each of the markets that we followed.

At this point we can take note of the fact that the price data that was collected in Figure 1.6 include the date, open, high, low, and close of each trading period. These four prices enable us to understand where the trading period (day) started and ended, and where the market traded during the period (the price range). These four prices, as we know, are what we need to create bar charts. The first person to create a price bar, depicting the trading range for a time period, with the opening price tick on the left and the closing tick on the right, was clearly innovative. Significant information is communicated in a single price bar.

Figure 1.6   General Motors price activity displayed in a text format by columns

Date	Open	High	Low	Close
February 20, 2002	$50.40	$52.45	$50.30	$52.28
February 21, 2002	$52.00	$52.80	$51.48	$51.73
February 22, 2002	$52.11	$53.60	$51.82	$53.11
February 25, 2002	$53.11	$55.80	$52.90	$55.48
February 26, 2002	$55.49	$55.66	$54.66	$54.94
February 27, 2002	$55.35	$55.35	$53.54	$53.77
February 28, 2002	$54.40	$54.40	$52.79	$52.98
March 1, 2002	$53.20	$55.20	$53.20	$54.97
March 4, 2002	$56.00	$59.19	$56.00	$58.70
March 5, 2002	$58.69	$59.72	$58.21	$58.61
March 6, 2002	$58.45	$60.44	$58.28	$59.92
March 7, 2002	$61.10	$61.60	$60.56	$61.41
March 8, 2002	$62.00	$62.01	$60.65	$60.71
March 11, 2002	$60.80	$61.69	$60.10	$61.14
March 12, 2002	$60.65	$61.30	$60.28	$61.00
March 13, 2002	$60.05	$60.43	$59.50	$59.90
March 14, 2002	$60.48	$60.48	$59.50	$59.90
March 15, 2002	$59.90	$61.06	$59.90	$60.75

Now that we can see that displaying price datum in a text format is extremely inefficient, we will analyze the revolutionary advancement that allows traders to understand and process price information easily and quickly. The traditional bar chart created from price datum displayed in Figure 1.6 can be seen in Figure 1.7.

It is easy to see that the traditional bar chart is able to communicate important information in a format that is easily understood and quickly processed. Price charts allow investors to know exactly what a market has done and what a market is doing at a glance. Making money in the markets is not only a function of making the correct decision, but also of acting upon that decision within a defined time window of opportunity. If decisions are not made quickly enough, opportunities can easily be missed. It is important that a market analysis technique created to define the valuation of a market have the same positive characteristics that traditional price charts contain. As we soon see, Value Charts are easy to read and condense information,

Figure 1.7   General Motors daily bar chart

Chart created with TradeStation® 2000i by Omega Research, Inc.

which allow traders to quickly interpret market activity in order to make quick trading decisions.

Traditional bar charts communicate the absolute behavior of a market while Value Charts communicate the relative behavior of a market. As we have learned, the terms *undervalued* and *overvalued* are relative terms. Value Charts have been developed to define the valuation of a market within a real-time market environment. Traders who do not possess these revolutionary market analysis tools will be at a significant disadvantage to those traders who do.

2

VALUE CHARTS

Although traditional bar charts are useful for referencing both the historical and current price activity of a market, they do not have the ability to chart price in such a way as to clearly define value. When utilizing traditional price charts, we are unable to identify the valuation of a market. Understanding the valuation of the current price level in a market is critical to trading successfully.

As we learned previously, the terms *overvalued* and *undervalued* are defined on a relative basis. When we are seeking to identify undervalued or overvalued price levels, it is necessary to reference the fair value price level. Therefore, instead of plotting price with respect to zero, it is necessary to plot price (open, high, low, and close) with respect to a moving (floating) axis, which is designed to represent fair value. Because fair value represents the price level where the majority of the buyers and sellers transact business, a carefully selected moving average of price activity should be representative of fair value in any market. This moving average is referred to as the *floating axis*.

Traditional bar charts state price activity relative to the zero axis. The first step in creating a Value Chart is to state price activity relative to the floating axis, which represents fair value. The bottom price chart in Figure 2.1 is plotted with respect to the floating axis. This chart is not a Value Chart, but rather a simple *relative price chart*. As

Figure 2.1   Daily AT&T price chart (top) and relative price chart (bottom)

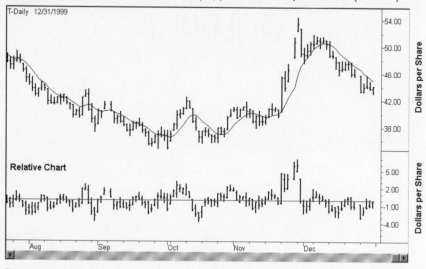

Chart created with TradeStation® 2000i by Omega Research, Inc.

we will soon see, Value Charts are a significantly improved version of relative price charts. In fact, relative charts in themselves have little usefulness.

The bottom chart in Figure 2.1 displays the price of AT&T stock on a relative basis. The AT&T relative price chart simply charts the open, high, low, and close with respect to a straight line version of the floating axis. This floating axis is also displayed as a curvy line on the top AT&T price chart. All things being equal, the further that price deviates to the upside away from the straight zero line, the more overbought, relatively speaking, it has become. The opposite holds true for deviations to the downside of the zero line. Imagine the line in the top chart in Figure 2.1 being pulled until it is straight. As this floating axis line is pulled straight, the price bars maintain their relationship with respect to this floating axis line. If the high of a particular day is two points above the curvy line in the top chart in Figure 2.1, then it will also be two points above the straight line in the bottom chart in Figure 2.1. The bottom relative chart simply presents price in a different format from the traditional absolute method of plotting price.

Table 2.1 displays some of the calculations used to generate the relative chart in Figure 2.1. The floating axis is simply calculated by averaging the median prices from the current price bars and most recent four price bars (five bars total). The median price is calculated as follows: (high + low)/2. After calculating this value for each price bar, we simply take the simple average of five bars to create our floating axis.

The relative high can be calculated by subtracting the floating axis from the high (high – floating axis = relative high). Using the

Table 2.1 Example calculations for generating the AT&T relative chart (Figure 2.1)

1	2	3	4	5	6	7	8	9	10
					Floating	Relative	Relative	Relative	Relative
Date	Open	High	Low	Close	Axis	Open	High	Low	Close
990830	40.51	41.39	38.67	39.19	41.23	–0.72	0.16	–2.56	–2.04
990831	39.19	39.51	37.35	38.19	40.91	–1.72	–1.40	–3.56	–2.72
990901	38.43	40.59	38.43	40.43	40.59	–2.16	0.00	–2.16	–0.16
990902	40.35	40.35	39.43	40.19	39.98	0.37	0.37	–0.55	0.21
990903	40.71	41.67	40.71	41.27	39.81	0.90	1.86	0.90	1.46
990907	41.27	41.71	40.39	40.39	40.01	1.26	1.70	0.38	0.38
990908	40.19	40.19	38.63	39.19	40.21	–0.02	–0.02	–1.58	–1.02
990909	39.19	39.67	38.51	39.51	40.13	–0.94	–0.46	–1.62	–0.62
990910	39.51	40.27	38.71	38.75	40.05	–0.54	0.22	–1.34	–1.30
990913	38.75	39.43	38.23	38.27	39.57	–0.82	–0.14	–1.34	–1.30
990914	38.27	38.35	37.39	37.51	38.94	–0.67	–0.59	–1.55	–1.43
990915	37.51	38.35	36.79	37.51	38.57	–1.06	–0.22	–1.78	–1.06
990916	37.55	38.79	37.55	38.51	38.39	–0.84	0.40	–0.84	0.12
990917	38.51	38.67	37.79	38.59	38.13	0.38	0.54	–0.34	0.46
990920	38.59	39.27	38.19	38.23	38.11	0.48	1.16	–0.08	0.12
990921	38.23	38.59	37.27	37.51	38.13	0.10	0.46	–0.86	–0.62
990922	37.51	37.71	36.67	37.19	38.05	–0.54	–0.34	–1.38	–0.86
990923	37.19	37.35	35.35	35.47	37.69	–0.50	–0.34	–2.34	–2.22
990924	35.47	36.27	35.19	35.59	37.19	–1.72	–0.92	–2.00	–1.60
990927	35.67	36.75	35.67	36.59	36.68	–1.01	0.07	–1.01	–0.09
990928	36.81	37.41	34.93	36.89	36.33	0.48	1.08	–1.40	0.56
990929	36.89	37.97	36.57	36.73	36.35	0.54	1.62	0.22	0.38
990930	36.73	37.49	36.01	36.73	36.43	0.30	1.06	–0.42	0.30

price data from 8/30/99, we can see this formula in action (high = 41.39, floating axis = 41.23, relative high = high – floating axis = 41.39 – 41.23 = 0.16). If necessary, take some time to become comfortable with this conversion of price into relative price by reviewing the data in Table 2.1.

The date, open, high, low, and close from the daily AT&T bar chart (as seen in Figure 2.1) are listed in the first five columns of Table 2.1. By utilizing the conversion formula in the preceding paragraph, we are able to calculate the relative price for each price bar. Simply repeat the conversion process for the open, high, low, and close to calculate the relative open, relative high, relative low, and relative close.

Now that we have the basic understanding of how to calculate a relative bar chart, we can view a relative chart for a different market, the soybean futures market (Figure 2.2). Although relative charts have no practical usefulness, it is important to understand where they fall short as a technical charting tool. This example, which displays a major bull market, will illustrate how volatility can significantly increase as this bull market progresses. Figure 2.2 displays a daily soybeans bar chart that is positioned directly above a daily soybeans relative bar chart. Once the normal bar chart prices were converted into relative prices, they were plotted directly below their corresponding normal price bars. Therefore, each traditional price bar is located directly above the corresponding relative price bar. Like the AT&T relative bar chart displayed in Figure 2.1, this new relative price chart reflects the relative movement of the soybeans market with respect to the floating axis. When the traditional price bars move further away from the floating axis in the top half of the chart, the relative price bars move further away from the zero line (straight line) in the bottom half of the chart.

Note that the curvy moving average line in the top chart, which represents the floating axis, is equivalent to the straightened zero line in the relative chart located on the bottom of Figure 2.2. Once again, imagine pulling the curvy moving average line (floating axis) in the top half of Figure 2.2 until it is straight. Just as before, this would transform the traditional chart into the relative chart. Upon a close inspection of the soybeans relative chart, it is evident that it was not

Figure 2.2   Daily soybeans price chart (top) and relative price chart (bottom)

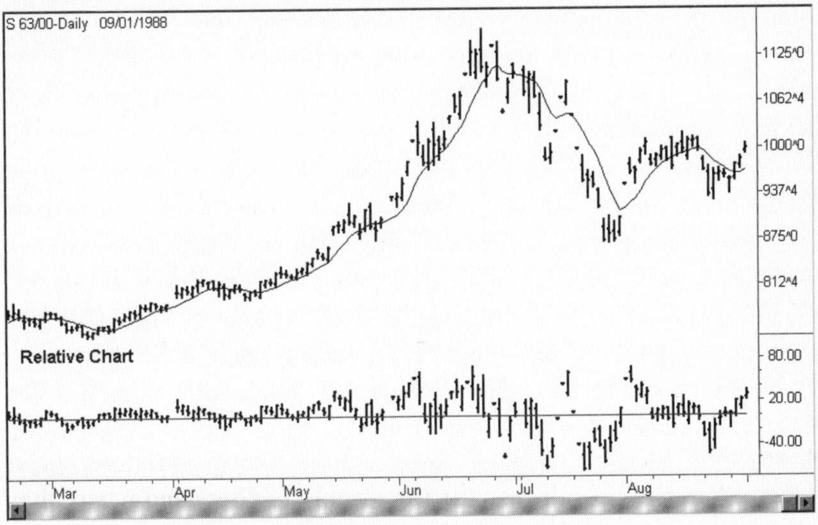

Chart created with TradeStation® 2000i by Omega Research, Inc.

very useful in identifying overbought or oversold market conditions because prices tended to deviate more from the zero line (floating axis line) as the market became more volatile. Note that in Figure 2.2, as the price of soybeans became much more volatile on the right side of the chart (June through August time frame) the relative price bars in the lower chart deviated much further from the zero axis. Remember, the zero axis in the relative chart (lower chart) represents the floating axis, which is the moving average in the traditional chart (top chart). The relative price chart clearly did not adjust to changing volatility conditions and therefore was of little value in defining the valuation of the soybeans market. Because the expected deviation from the zero line is always changing with market volatility, relative charts will not be effective in defining the valuation of any market.

In order for a relative chart to be useful in identifying overbought and oversold price levels, it would have to have the ability to adapt to changing market volatility. The need for the relative chart (displayed in Figure 2.2) to be defined in terms of volatility was the driving force in developing a dynamic volatility unit instead of using a static price unit. This new dynamic volatility unit would be the breakthrough that would allow relative charts to be transformed into Value Charts, which are effective in defining relative overbought and oversold price levels as market volatility changes over time. As you probably have guessed, these new volatility adjusted relative charts were named *Value Charts.*

Market volatility can be defined as "a measure or expectation of how much a market can move over time." Higher volatility equates to more price movement, whereas lower volatility equates to less price movement. For example, if the weekly trading range of Microsoft was $4 per share last week and the weekly trading range is $8 this week, we would conclude that the volatility of Microsoft stock has increased. Typically, the market volatility is correlated to the absolute price level of a market. A stock that is trading near the $10 price level might be expected to have weekly price fluctuations of $1, whereas a stock trading near the $100 price level might be expected to have weekly price fluctuations of $10.

The correlation between absolute price and market volatility can be illustrated in another way. When a person is going to purchase a house, he or she will typically submit an offer below the asking price of the house that they are interested in purchasing. The offer will typically be a certain percentage below the asking price. A person looking to bid on a $100,000 house might submit a bid of $95,000, which represents a 5 percent discount off the asking price. On the other hand, a person who is looking to bid on a $1 million house might submit a bid of $950,000, which also represents a 5 percent discount off the asking price. The magnitude of the discount often goes up along with the amount of the asking prices. It would be ludicrous for the buyer of the $100,000 house to mimic the buyer of the $1 million house and ask for a $50,000 discount off the sales price. A $50,000 discount off the price of the $1 million house represents a savings of 5 percent to the buyer, whereas a discount of $50,000 off the price of the $100,000 house represents a savings of 50 percent to the buyer. After examining this case, it is easy to see that price fluctuations in a market tend to be correlated to the absolute price level.

VALUE CHARTS

As the price of a market climbs to higher price levels, the volatility almost always increases. There tends to be a high correlation between the magnitude of the price fluctuations around fair value and the absolute price level in a market. Given this observation, it is necessary for relative price charts, as stated previously, to have the ability to adjust to changing volatility. In order to accomplish what relative charts are unable to accomplish, Value Charts are defined in terms of a dynamic volatility unit. These dynamic volatility units allow Value Charts to effectively adjust to changing market volatility. We can now review the AT&T chart displayed in Figure 2.1 with a Value Chart instead of a relative chart.

The Value Chart at the bottom of Figure 2.3 displays the daily price activity of AT&T on a relative, volatility-adjusted basis. The relative bar chart that was displayed in Figure 2.1 had units of dollars per share. The AT&T Value Chart in Figure 2.3 uses dynamic volatility units as the units to define price movement or price deviations. As you

Figure 2.3   Daily AT&T price chart (top) and Value Chart (bottom)

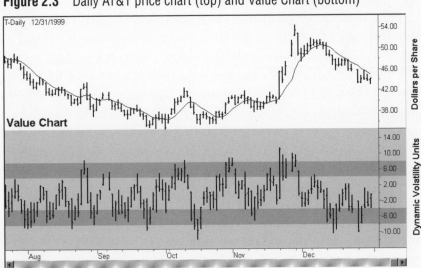

Chart created with TradeStation® 2000i by Omega Research, Inc.

can see, there are four horizontal lines, which separate the different shaded zones, plotted on the Value Chart of AT&T stock. These different zones are used to identify different degrees of overbought or oversold trading activity. For example, the range between the two inner lines (between –4 and +4) represents fair value. A thorough explanation of the different valuation zones is given later in this chapter and in Chapter 3.

The results from the calculations used to generate the Value Chart for AT&T in Figure 2.3 are displayed in Table 2.2. We utilize the same steps that were used to generate a relative chart and, in addition, add one more mathematical step to adjust price to changing volatility. As before, the relative high can be calculated by subtracting the floating axis from the high (high – floating axis = relative high). The Value Chart high can then be calculated by dividing the relative high (or relative price) by the dynamic volatility unit. Using the price data from 8/30/99, we can see this formula in action by using the following values (high = 41.39, floating axis = 41.23, volatility unit = 0.42). The Value Chart high = (high – floating axis)/(volatility unit) = (41.39 – 41.23)/(0.42) = 0.38). If necessary, take some time to become comfortable with this conversion of relative price into Value Chart price by reviewing Table 2.2.

The dynamic volatility unit can be calculated by first taking a five day average of the daily range. The range of a single day is defined as high – low. After calculating the five day average, this average is then multiplied by 0.20, or 1/5. The dynamic volatility unit (volatility unit) can be calculated as follows by using the high and low values from the first five bars.

Volatility Unit (9/3/99)
$$= ((41.39 - 38.67) + (39.51 - 37.35) + (40.59 - 38.43)$$
$$+ (40.35 - 39.43) + (41.67 - 40.71))/5 \times 0.20$$
$$= 0.357 \text{ or } 0.36 \text{ (rounded)}$$

Note that the volatility unit for September 3, 1999, which can be found in the fifth row and the seventh column, was indeed 0.36. Repeat this process to calculate the remaining volatility units for each additional trading day.

Table 2.2 Example calculations for generating the AT&T Value Chart (Figure 2.3)

1	2	3	4	5	6	7	8	9	10	11
Date	Open	High	Low	Close	Floating Axis	Volatility Unit	V Chart Open	V Chart High	V Chart Low	V Chart Close
990830	40.51	41.39	38.67	39.19	41.23	0.42	-1.71	0.38	-6.08	-4.85
990831	39.19	39.51	37.35	38.19	40.91	0.46	-3.76	-3.06	-7.80	-5.96
990901	38.43	40.59	38.43	40.43	40.59	0.44	-4.92	-0.01	-4.92	-0.37
990902	40.35	40.35	39.43	40.19	39.98	0.44	0.85	0.85	-1.25	0.48
990903	40.71	41.67	40.71	41.27	39.81	0.36	2.52	5.21	2.52	4.09
990907	41.27	41.71	40.39	40.39	40.01	0.30	4.18	5.64	1.25	1.25
990908	40.19	40.19	38.63	39.19	40.21	0.28	-0.07	-0.07	-5.71	-3.68
990909	39.19	39.67	38.51	39.51	40.13	0.24	-3.95	-1.93	-6.82	-2.60
990910	39.51	40.27	38.71	38.75	40.05	0.26	-2.04	0.85	-5.09	-4.94
990913	38.75	39.43	38.23	38.27	39.57	0.27	-3.03	-0.53	-4.94	-4.79
990914	38.27	38.35	37.39	37.51	38.94	0.26	-2.59	-2.28	-6.01	-5.54
990915	37.51	38.35	36.79	37.51	38.57	0.26	-4.11	-0.85	-6.91	-4.11
990916	37.55	38.79	37.55	38.51	38.39	0.26	-3.21	1.55	-3.21	0.48
990917	38.51	38.67	37.79	38.59	38.13	0.23	1.61	2.29	-1.47	1.95
990920	38.59	39.27	38.19	38.23	38.11	0.23	2.08	5.05	0.33	0.51
990921	38.23	38.59	37.27	37.51	38.13	0.24	0.43	1.91	-3.52	-2.53
990922	37.51	37.71	36.67	37.19	38.05	0.22	-2.43	-1.53	-6.21	-3.87
990923	37.19	37.35	35.35	35.47	37.69	0.25	-1.96	-1.33	-9.24	-8.77
990924	35.47	36.27	35.19	35.59	37.19	0.26	-6.58	-3.51	-7.65	-6.12
990927	35.67	36.75	35.67	36.59	36.68	0.26	-3.88	0.26	-3.88	-0.35
990928	36.81	37.41	34.93	36.89	36.33	0.31	1.56	3.52	-4.56	1.82
990929	36.89	37.97	36.57	36.73	36.35	0.32	1.69	5.05	0.70	1.10
990930	36.73	37.49	36.01	36.73	36.43	0.30	1.01	3.54	-1.38	1.01

As before, the date, open, high, low, and close of the daily AT&T bar chart are listed in the first five columns of Table 2.2. By utilizing the floating axis formula, we are able to calculate the floating axis in column 6. By utilizing the dynamic volatility unit formula, we are able to calculate the dynamic volatility unit (volatility unit) values in column 7. The dynamic volatility unit is designed to adjust Value Chart prices to changing volatility.

Now that we understand how a Value Chart is generated, we can observe its effectiveness by looking at the bull market in soybeans displayed in Figure 2.4. Unlike the relative chart, the Value Chart displays price on a relative, volatility-adjusted basis.

As you can see, the daily soybeans Value Chart in Figure 2.4 is significantly different from the relative price chart displayed in Figure 2.2. You can see in Figure 2.4 that the Value Chart is effective in adjusting to different volatility levels in the soybeans bull market. It is not uncommon for markets to dramatically increase in volatility when they reach higher price levels. In fact, we all know that the volatility characteristics of every free market tend to change over time as prices

Figure 2.4   Daily soybeans bar chart above a daily soybeans Value Chart

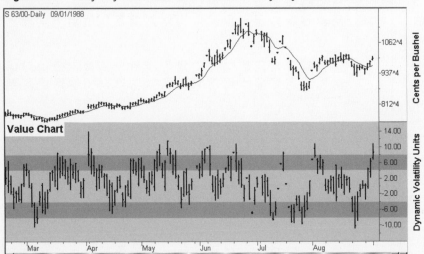

Chart created with TradeStation® 2000i by Omega Research, Inc.

change. A Value Chart has the ability to adapt to different levels of volatility in any standardized free market. This allows Value Charts to effectively define overbought and oversold price levels. In other words, as volatility changes, the point deviation from the zero line in the Value Chart that would constitute a certain degree of being overbought or oversold would theoretically remain the same. Therefore, Value Charts can effectively identify overbought and oversold price levels in the soybeans bull market in March 1988 (when market volatility is lower) just as well as it can effectively identify overbought and oversold price levels in August 1988 (when market volatility is significantly higher).

Now we can begin to further understand how to use Value Charts when we are analyzing markets. The Value Chart is usually positioned directly below the corresponding price chart for a particular market. The Value Chart can also be displayed on its own, without the traditional bar chart.

Figure 2.5 displays both the Value Chart and the relative chart di-

Figure 2.5 Soybeans bar chart over a Value Chart (middle) and a relative chart (bottom)

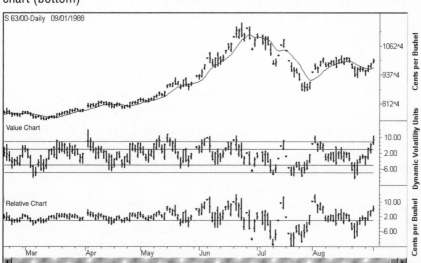

Chart created with TradeStation® 2000i by Omega Research, Inc.

rectly below a daily bar chart of the 1988 soybeans bull market. During the February–March time period the relative chart deviated from 0 +17 cents to the upside and –17 cents to the downside. During the July time period, when soybeans experienced peak volatility, the relative chart deviated from 0 +66 cents to the upside and –77 cents to the downside. These relative chart values represent a 390 percent increase in upside deviations and a 450 percent increase in downside deviations from the mean (zero) when the soybeans market dramatically increased in volatility from the earlier stages of the bull market to the climax of the bull market.

On the other hand, during the February–March time period the Value Chart deviated from 0 +9.7 dynamic volatility units to the upside and –10.2 dynamic volatility units to the downside. During the July time period, when soybeans experienced peak volatility, the Value Chart deviated from 0 +10.7 dynamic volatility units to the upside and –9.52 dynamic volatility units to the downside. The Value Chart was successful in adjusting to dramatically increased volatility in the soybeans market over the course of the 1988 bull market.

The ability of Value Charts to adjust to changing market volatility allows us to define overbought and oversold price levels even when market volatility changes dramatically over time. Now that we have seen that Value Charts can adjust to increasing volatility within a single bull market, we can go on and test how well Value Charts can adapt to the steadily increasing volatility as seen in the S&P 500 futures market over two decades. A major bull market lasting approximately 20 years in the S&P 500 futures market results in an increase of more than 400 percent in the value of this stock index. This results in a dramatic increase in market volatility and price swings, which create the perfect testing ground for the Value Charts and Price Action Profile concepts. Later in this book we introduce Price Action Profile as a complement to Value Charts.

The charts in Figure 2.6 represent the S&P 500 futures market price activity in the early 1980s, when the stock index traded around the 500 point level. On the other hand, the charts in Figure 2.7 represent the S&P 500 futures market price activity in the late 1990s, when the stock index traded around the 1,400 point level.

Figure 2.6 S&P 500 bar chart in 1982 over a Value Chart and a relative chart

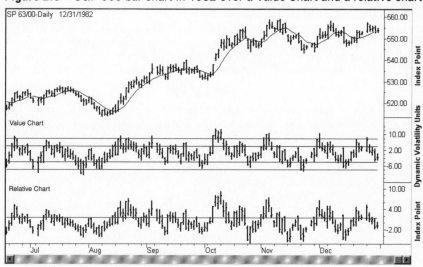

Chart created with TradeStation® 2000i by Omega Research, Inc.

Notice in Figure 2.6 that the S&P 500 relative chart during 1982 experienced deviations from 0 as high as +9.0 and as low as –6.1. However, 17 years later in 1999 when the S&P 500 market was trading at much higher price levels and much higher volatility levels (Figure 2.7), the S&P 500 relative chart experienced deviations from 0 as high as +59.9 and as low as –54.0. In this example, the market volatility increased significantly over the course of almost two decades. Now, as we examine Figure 2.6, we note that the Value Chart experienced deviations from zero as high as +12.5 and as low as –10.3, whereas in 1999 (Figure 2.7), the Value Chart experienced deviations from zero as high as +11.0 and as low as –11.0. The Value Charts tool was successful in adapting to the slowly increasing levels of volatility in the S&P 500 futures markets.

Incredibly, the Value Chart in Figure 2.5 has the same price scale, represented in terms of dynamic volatility units, that the Value Charts have in both Figure 2.6 and Figure 2.7. Value Charts are able to adapt to changing market volatility and, at the same time, are able

Figure 2.7   S&P 500 bar chart in 1999 over a Value Chart and a relative chart

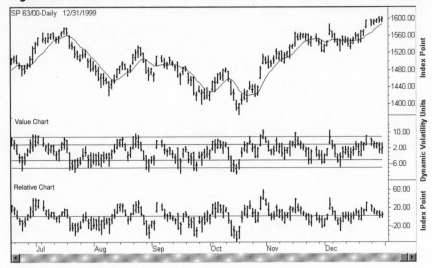

Chart created with TradeStation® 2000i by Omega Research, Inc.

to chart price activity from any standardized and liquid free market in the world.

As you will see later in this book, this fact is very significant because you can now design trading systems that enter or exit markets at Value Chart price levels. Because Value Charts works in the same manner across every market by using the same universal overbought and oversold point scale, trading strategies no longer have to be revised to accommodate each unique market.

HOW TO READ VALUE CHARTS

As we have learned, Value Charts are effective in normalizing deviations from fair value in different volatility environments, which enables them to define the valuation of a market. This basically means that a deviation of +4 Value Chart units, which represents a specific degree of overbought prices, should very nearly equal a deviation of +4 Value Chart units in a totally different volatility environment. When we are inspecting a Value Chart, it is important to understand that the closer prices are to zero, the more closely prices represent fair value. On the other hand, the further away prices trade from zero, the more overbought or the more oversold it becomes. We can now take time to inspect a traditional bar chart of Hewlett-Packard along with its corresponding Value Chart (see Figure 2.8).

Because markets tend to experience choppy price action more often than they trend, it is necessary to rely on Value Charts to help locate optimal entry and exit points. Notice that many of the significantly overbought (down arrows) and significantly oversold (up arrows) points on the Value Chart represent short-term highs and short-term lows in the price of Hewlett-Packard stock. Not only is the Value Chart effective in identifying the extreme price bars, it also is effective in identifying the portion of the extreme bars that extend into the significantly overbought and significantly oversold price levels. The ability to identify the portion of the price bars that extends into the extreme overbought and oversold zones is one of the most powerful features of Value Charts (see Figure 2.9).

Figure 2.8 Daily Hewlett-Packard price chart (top) and Value Chart (bottom)

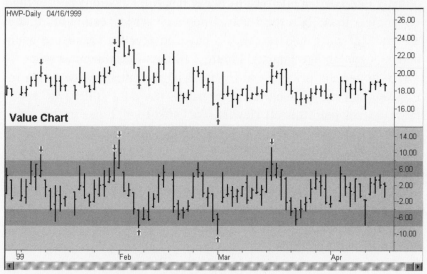

Chart created with TradeStation® 2000i by Omega Research, Inc.

Figure 2.9   Extreme price levels identified by Value Charts

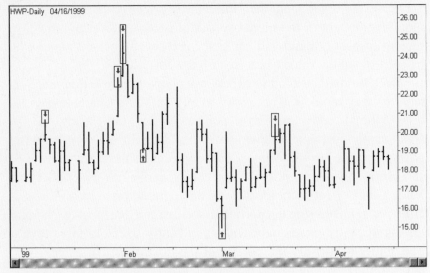

Chart created with TradeStation® 2000i by Omega Research, Inc.

The extreme valuation levels (extremely overbought and extremely oversold) are defined by Value Chart fluctuations greater than +8 and less than –8, respectively. Upon a closer inspection of Figures 2.8 and 2.9, an astute eye would have observed a premature overbought signal in late January. Figure 2.10 identifies this price point.

Although the price bar in Figure 2.10 identified by the down arrow was not the ultimate short-term top, it would still have been a fairly decent point to sell Hewlett-Packard stock. Later in this book we learn some practical rules on how to increase our odds when trading with Value Charts. When analyzing the Value Charts in Figures 2.8 and 2.10, it is important to remember that the Value Chart price range between the two middle lines represents fair value. As we begin to learn about Price Action Profile in Chapter 3, we begin to understand the reasoning behind how fair value, overbought, and oversold valuation levels are identified.

Now that we understand how Value Charts were developed, we can take time to learn how to read them. For now, we focus on

Figure 2.10   Premature overbought signal identified by Value Charts

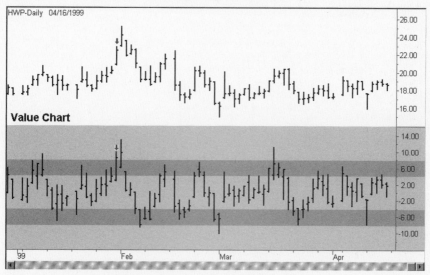

Chart created with TradeStation® 2000i by Omega Research, Inc.

the most basic application of Value Charts. Take time to review Figure 2.11.

The most basic configuration of a charting screen that includes Value Charts is displayed in Figure 2.11. Note that the conventional price chart is positioned directly above the Value Chart. It is also important to note that this screen displays price in the two primary formats, on an absolute basis with the traditional bar chart and on a relative basis with the Value Chart. Each of these types of charts communicates different information about the markets and each chart can be displayed individually if desired.

We can now examine the Value Chart displayed independently of the traditional price chart, in Figure 2.12. The Value Chart is organized into five primary valuation zones including significantly overbought, moderately overbought, fair value, moderately oversold, and significantly oversold. An explanation is provided for the methodology used to define each of these valuation zones (ranges) in Chapter 3. We can now take time to view the five valuation zones labeled on the Value Chart that appears in Figure 2.12. It contains the United

Figure 2.11   United Technologies chart (top) above a Value Chart (bottom)

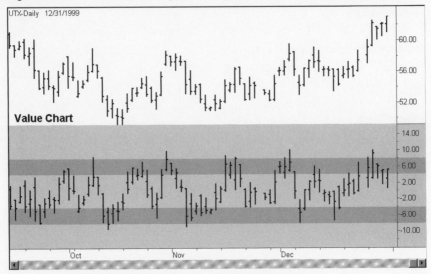

Chart created with TradeStation® 2000i by Omega Research, Inc.

Figure 2.12   United Technologies Value Chart

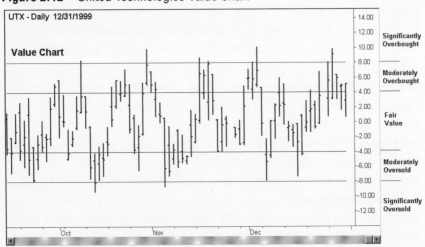

Chart created with TradeStation® 2000i by Omega Research, Inc.

Technologies Value Chart displayed in Figure 2.11 independently of the traditional bar chart.

For the Value Chart displayed in Figure 2.12, *fair value* is defined as "the range between –4 and +4." This range should contain most of the trading activity over time. The Value Chart price ranges extending from –8 to –4 and +4 to +8 are the moderately oversold and moderately overbought ranges, respectively. Last, the Value Chart price range located below –8 represents the significantly oversold zone and the Value Chart price range located above +8 represents the significantly overbought zone. Therefore, a Value Chart closing price of +6.34 would be considered moderately overbought. A Value Chart low (of the day) of –9.2 would be considered significantly oversold. A Value Chart opening price of 2.2 would be considered fair value.

A simple review of the Value Chart price activity in Figure 2.11 reveals that many of the extreme short-term highs and lows that appeared on the traditional bar chart corresponded with price bars that traded in the significantly overbought and significantly oversold price ranges in the Value Chart. The United Technologies Value Chart was able to identify and define these short-term extremes during the trading sessions, not after the fact. Having possession of a tool that enhances a trader's ability to identify short-term market tops and bottoms is extremely valuable. Common sense would dictate that we, at a very minimum, should not responsibly buy into a market that is trading in the significantly overbought price zone or sell into a market that is trading in the significantly oversold price zone.

Consider the top portion of the daily trading range of United Technologies stock on October 29, 1999, as identified by the small down arrow in Figure 2.13. It is clear that the top section of this bar is trading in the significantly overbought Value Chart price range because it penetrated above the +8 Value Chart price level. There were unfortunate buyers who bought at these price levels and prudent sellers who sold at these price levels. If these buyers had known that the United Technologies stock they had purchased was significantly overvalued, they could have waited for more attractive price levels and, in this

Figure 2.13 United Technologies chart (top) above a Value Chart (bottom)

Chart created with TradeStation® 2000i by Omega Research, Inc.

case, had the opportunity to save themselves up to $8 per share over the next several trading sessions.

It is important to understand that short-term (daily) Value Charts do not shed insight into the long-term direction of the market. They are, however, very useful for identifying both attractive and unattractive short-term market entry and exit price levels. During the months of October, November, and December the prices of United Technologies stock experienced fluctuations of up to 15 percent of the price of the stock. Because most markets experience these significant price oscillations over time, it is essential that investors attempt to enter or exit markets at attractive price levels. The unfortunate buyer(s) who entered the United Technologies stock at the significantly overbought price level identified in Figure 2.13 experienced a loss of greater than 11 percent over the following nine trading sessions because they entered the market at a significantly overbought price level.

Value Charts allow us to understand the valuation of any standardized, liquid market. They are useful for analyzing stocks, bonds, currencies, and futures markets. The U.S. Treasury notes futures market at the Chicago Board of Trade serves as another example of a market that can be evaluated with Value Charts. It is interesting to note that a one-point price move is worth $1,000 per contract in the 10-year Treasury notes market, whereas a one-point move in domestic stocks is worth only $1 per share. Even though the dollar value of a one-point move in any market under consideration may change, the valuation zones on a Value Chart remain the same. In other words, we would expect to define fair value as the Value Charts price zone extending from –4 to +4 for markets ranging from Microsoft stock to soybean futures.

Once again, we can see in Figure 2.14 that price bars penetrating the significantly overbought or significantly oversold Value Chart levels often coincided with short-term highs and lows in the 10-year Treasury notes futures market. In this example, Value Charts again serve as a powerful tool in revealing attractive price levels to enter the 10-year Treasury notes market.

Figure 2.14   U.S. Treasury note futures chart (top) above a Value Chart (bottom)

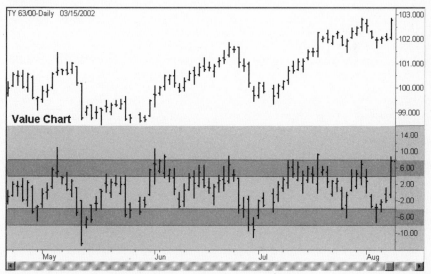

Chart created with TradeStation® 2000i by Omega Research, Inc.

Although a Value Chart is an extremely useful standalone trading tool, it is significantly enhanced by a Price Action Profile. Just as Value Charts are powerful tools that shed insight into the valuation of a market, Price Action Profile allows traders to identify the exact degree by which a market is overbought or oversold. Chapter 3 focuses on the development and applications of Price Action Profile. Chapter 2 touches on the most basic applications of Value Charts. Other remaining chapters in this book outline more in-depth applications of Value Charts.

Value Charts are designed to identify the valuation of a market. Having the ability to identify short-term undervalued price levels allows us to identify optimal buying opportunities in the markets. Value Charts are powerful market analysis tools that no trader should be without. In Chapter 3, we observe how Price Action Profile is used to both complement and validate Value Charts.

3

PRICE ACTION PROFILE

In the previous chapter we observed that a Value Chart can be a powerful market analysis tool in identifying the valuation of a standardized market. The ability of Value Charts to adapt to changing volatility conditions in any market along with the ability to function effectively across an array of significantly different markets makes Value Charts a market analysis tool that every trader should have. However, Value Charts can be powerfully enhanced with Price Action Profiles. A *Price Action Profile* is simply "a profile that describes, or plots, the historical price behavior of a Value Chart." Price Action Profiles can define how frequently a Value Chart has traded above, below, or within any given Value Chart sector.

CREATING A PRICE ACTION PROFILE

Recall that a Price Action Profile reflects the distribution of the Value Chart price activity. When creating a Price Action Profile, the Value Chart bars are simply piled up on one side, preferably on the left, of the Value Chart. The figures that follow demonstrate the step-by-step process of creating a Price Action Profile from a Value Chart. Ignore the thickness of the bars and focus on how they pile up, or accumulate, on the left side of the Value Charts.

Figure 3.1a contains a Price Action Profile constructed from just one Value Chart price bar. The accumulating of many price bars is what often generates a bell curve shape in a Price Action Profile. Observe the addition of a second, third, and fourth Value Chart price bar in Figure 3.1b, Figure 3.1c, and Figure 3.1d. Note how the additional price bars enhance the shape of the Price Action Profile in Figure 3.1d.

Understanding how a Price Action Profile is generated is fairly simple. When you examine Figure 3.1d, you can count how frequently

Figure 3.1a Constructing a Price Action Profile

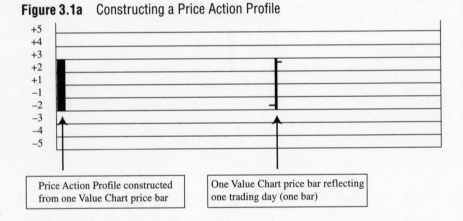

Figure 3.1b Constructing a Price Action Profile

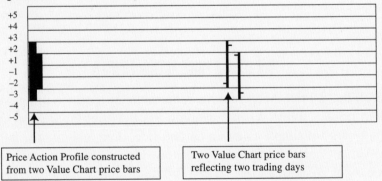

Figure 3.1c Constructing a Price Action Profile

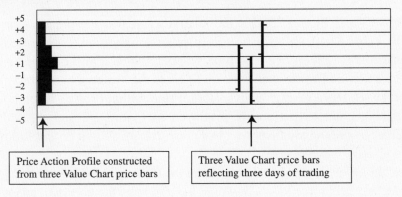

Price Action Profile constructed from three Value Chart price bars

Three Value Chart price bars reflecting three days of trading

Figure 3.1d Construction of a Price Action Profile

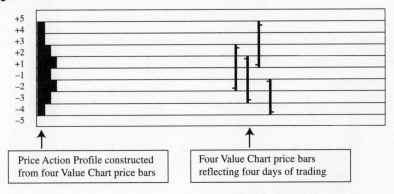

Price Action Profile constructed from four Value Chart price bars

Four Value Chart price bars reflecting four days of trading

each of the trading bars trades within each of the Value Chart price intervals. For example, the first three bars in the Value Chart trade within the (0 to) +1 Value Chart interval. Notice that the Price Action Profile reflects this by having three layers in the +1 Value Chart interval. As price bars are added to the Value Chart, the Price Action Profile will continue to accumulate the Value Chart bars and eventually form the shape of a bell curve. It is important to understand that a Price Action Profile simply reflects the frequency that a Value Chart trades within each Value Chart interval (sector).

VALIDATING VALUE CHARTS WITH PRICE ACTION PROFILE

Recall from Figure 2.2 that the relative chart was the predecessor to the Value Chart. Price Action Profiles were important in determining that relative charts were of little practical value. On the other hand, Price Action Profiles substantiate the fact that Value Charts are valid and useful as a market analysis tool. Price Action Profiles of both the relative chart as previously displayed in Figure 2.2 and the Value Chart as previously displayed in Figure 2.4 are shown on the following pages.

In order for a relative chart to be useful in identifying overbought and oversold price levels, it would have to have the ability to adapt to changing market volatility. The profile in Figure 3.2 generated from

Figure 3.2   Frequency histogram of daily soybeans relative chart

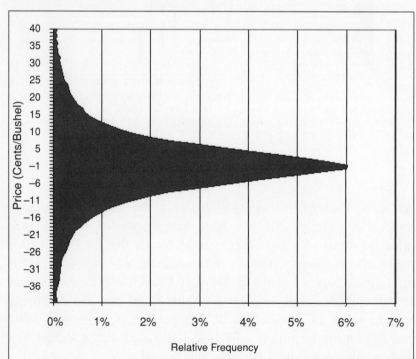

the soybeans relative price chart in Figure 3.3 is of no statistical value because of its thornlike shape. This is understandable given that relative prices are always in a constant state of becoming more or less volatile along with the price. In a relative chart, the reference levels that define different degrees of overbought or oversold price levels are always changing. Therefore, historical relative price activity is of little value because historical volatility is always changing and is most likely different from the present market volatility. We need to be able to compare apples with apples when defining different degrees of overbought and oversold price levels, and relative charts simply do not allow us to do this.

Now we need to generate a Price Action Profile for the Value Chart displayed in Figure 3.4. The chart in Figure 3.4 displays only about nine months of price data. We are interested in building a profile from much more extensive Value Chart price activity. Again, building a profile simply involves stacking or sliding all the Value Chart daily price bars to the left of the screen. In this example, we evaluate approximately 30 years of price data as we develop this

Figure 3.3   Daily soybeans bar chart above a daily soybeans relative chart

Chart created with TradeStation® 2000i by Omega Research, Inc.

Figure 3.4   Daily soybeans bar chart above a daily soybeans Value Chart

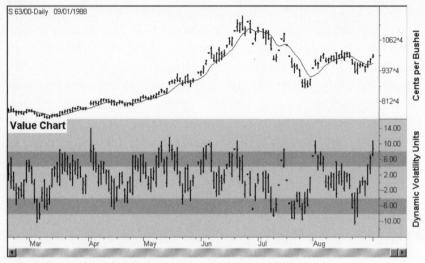

Chart created with TradeStation® 2000i by Omega Research, Inc.

frequency diagram or bell curve of market activity (displayed in Figure 3.5). The previous profile generated from nonvolatility adjusted price intervals (relative chart) was of little use from a statistical standpoint. However, as you can see, this new profile, which we have named a *Price Action Profile*, was derived from the Value Chart price data and is statistically valid in that it closely resembles the shape of a normal mound-shaped bell curve. This is very significant in that normal mound-shaped bell curves reflect a statistically normal distribution of behavior. By establishing what historical Value Chart price behavior has done, we are able to predict with a fairly high degree of accuracy what future Value Chart price behavior should do. In other words, we can expect the future Price Action Profile to closely resemble the past Price Action Profile. This is possible because Value Charts are effective in adapting to changing market volatility. We further examine this subject in upcoming pages.

As you can see in Figure 3.5, the Price Action Profile resembles a bell curve, whereas the profile generated by the nonvolatility adjusted relative price chart in Figure 3.3 resembles a thorn. Because the Price

Figure 3.5   Price Action Profile generated from the daily soybeans Value
Chart

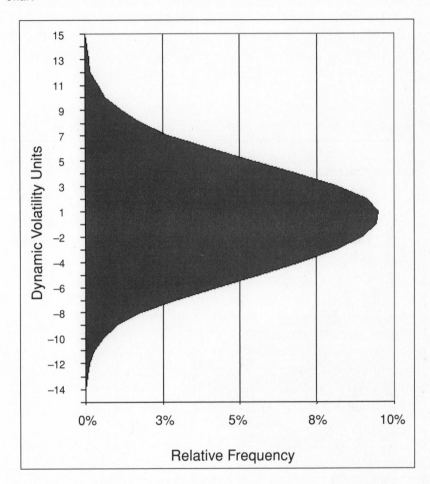

Action Profile in Figure 3.5 closely resembles a normal bell curve, we
can now make inferences about the population (future soybeans
prices) by using rules of statistics. As you know, having insight on the
future behavior of any market can lead to trading profits.

By further analyzing the Price Action Profile in Figure 3.5, we
can quantify the frequency in which the soybeans Value Chart has

traded in each Value Chart price interval. This analysis is displayed in
Figure 3.6.

When analyzing Figure 3.6, it is important to note that normal (or
mound-shaped) bell curves tend to have approximately 68 percent of
their distribution between ±1 standard deviation, approximately 95
percent of their distribution between ±2 standard deviations, and ap-

Figure 3.6   Price Action Profile analysis from a daily soybeans Value Chart

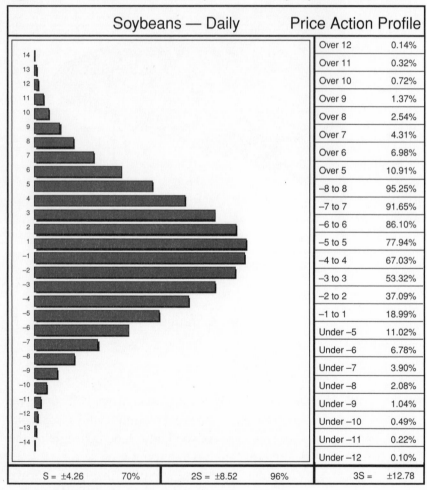

Soybeans — Daily	Price Action Profile	
	Over 12	0.14%
	Over 11	0.32%
	Over 10	0.72%
	Over 9	1.37%
	Over 8	2.54%
	Over 7	4.31%
	Over 6	6.98%
	Over 5	10.91%
	−8 to 8	95.25%
	−7 to 7	91.65%
	−6 to 6	86.10%
	−5 to 5	77.94%
	−4 to 4	67.03%
	−3 to 3	53.32%
	−2 to 2	37.09%
	−1 to 1	18.99%
	Under −5	11.02%
	Under −6	6.78%
	Under −7	3.90%
	Under −8	2.08%
	Under −9	1.04%
	Under −10	0.49%
	Under −11	0.22%
	Under −12	0.10%

S = ±4.26	70%	2S = ±8.52	96%	3S =	±12.78

proximately all the distribution within ±3 standard deviations (see Figure 3.7). Because this is an accepted convention in statistics, a rule that is observed to work in practice, it has been called the Empirical Rule (Figure 3.7). The soybean Price Action Profile has approximately 70 percent of its distribution between ±1 standard deviation (S = 4.26), approximately 96 percent of its distribution between ±2 standard deviations (2S = 8.52), and approximately 100 percent of its distribution within ±3 standard deviations (3S = 12.78).

The exact shape of the bell curve is not important because the rule will adequately describe the variability for mound-shaped distributions of data encountered in real life. As you can see when reviewing Figure 3.7, the relative frequencies of mound-shaped distributions are largest near the center of the distribution and tend to decrease as you move toward the distribution tails. Because the ±4 Value Chart range so closely resembles the ±1 standard deviation range and the ±8 Value Chart range so closely resembles the ±2 standard deviation range on most Price Action Profiles, we primarily utilize these Value Chart ranges instead of standard deviation measurements.

When we once again refer to Figure 3.6, we can observe an abundance of useful information about soybeans Value Charts from the Price Action Profile analysis of the soybeans market. For example, we can see from the column to the right of the Price Action Profile chart that the soybeans Value Chart trades only above the +12 Value Chart price level 0.14 percent of the time (see Figure 3.8).

We can see that 37.09 percent of the soybeans Value Chart prices trades within the ±2 Value Chart range (see Figure 3.9). We can also see that the soybeans Value Chart trades only below the –8 Value Chart level 2.08 percent of the time (see Figure 3.10).

For the remainder of this book, we use Value Charts with lines located at the ±4 and the ±8 Value Chart price levels. This is primarily because the approximately represent the ±1 standard deviation (approximately 68 percent of Value Chart trading activity) and the ±2 standard deviation (approximately 95 percent of Value Chart trading activity) ranges, respectively.

Figure 3.7   The Empirical Rule describing a normal (mound-shaped) bell curve

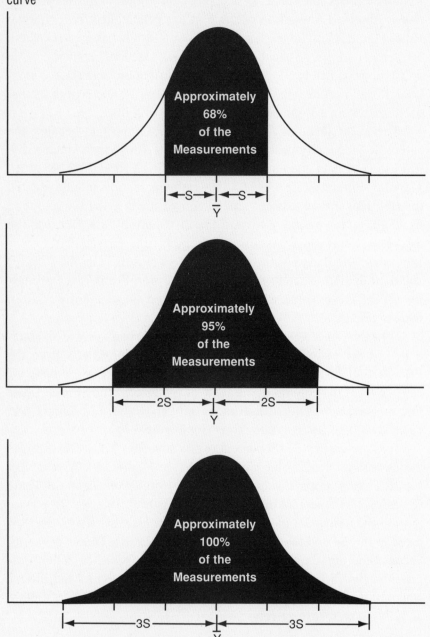

Figure 3.8   Daily soybeans Value Chart with a +12 Value Chart line

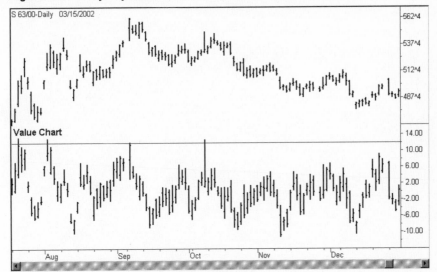

Chart created with TradeStation® 2000i by Omega Research, Inc.

Figure 3.9   Daily soybeans Value Chart with ±2 Value Chart lines

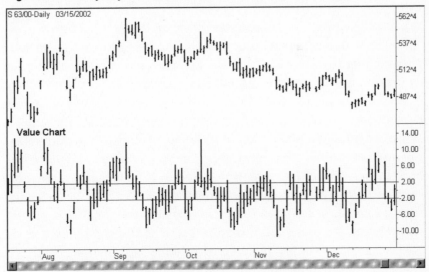

Chart created with TradeStation® 2000i by Omega Research, Inc.

Figure 3.10   Daily soybeans Value Chart with a −8 Value Chart line

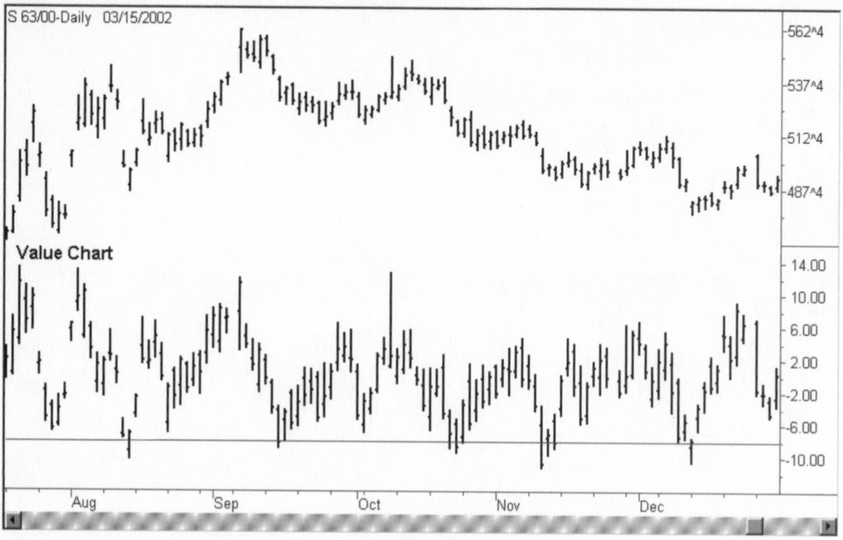

Chart created with TradeStation® 2000i by Omega Research, Inc.

THE FREQUENCY HISTOGRAM AS A VALUABLE MARKET ANALYSIS TOOL

Statistics have been a valuable tool in many different areas of business. The U.S. government is constantly releasing statistics about subjects ranging from crime to average life expectancies. Manufacturing companies rely on statistics to monitor quality control issues in their manufacturing plants. The objective of statistics is to make an inference about a population based on information contained in a sample. When we refer to a population in the arena of statistics, we are referring to the set of all measurements of interest. A *sample* might be defined as "a subset of measurements obtained from the population."

The value of a frequency histogram that reflects the behavior from a sample, which should closely resemble the population, is that it is information presented in a form that is easily and quickly readable. Charts are simply pictures of information. Charts effectively condense information and are easily comprehended by both the novice and the veteran alike. Our goal as traders is to have insight into how the market is behaving at present so that we might be able to predict how the market is likely to behave in the future. In short, we hope that the Price Action Profile generated from the sample data will allow us to make an accurate inference about the population of price data. The characteristics of the past population of price data should closely mirror the characteristics of the future population of price data, and thus allow traders to predict future price behavior with a defined degree of accuracy.

VALIDATING VALUE CHARTS WITH PRICE ACTION PROFILES

The key characteristic that enables Value Charts to be useful over time is their ability to adjust to changing volatility environments. The dynamic volatility units allow a Value Chart to adapt to changing market volatility and therefore remain effective in quantifying fair value, relative overbought, or relative oversold Value Chart price levels.

Value Charts as a market analysis tool needs to pass two important tests in order for us to place confidence in it as a valid tool. First, we would expect Price Action Profiles generated from the Value Charts of several different markets to be fairly similar. Second, we would expect that a Price Action Profile generated from one decade of price data to be fairly similar to a Price Action Profile generated from another decade of price data for any given market, assuming that the decades did not represent two vastly different directions in price trends (bull market versus bear market). As you know, market volatility can change dramatically over time in any given market. The second test will verify that Value Charts can effectively adapt and remain effective when market volatility changes over time. The tests that we examine use the most commonly used bar chart, the daily bar chart.

COMPARING THE PRICE ACTION PROFILES OF DIFFERENT MARKETS

The first test that needs to be performed on the Value Chart market analysis concept is to generate a Price Action Profile from the Value Charts of several different markets and compare the results. The assumption is that the Price Action Profiles generated from several different markets will be very similar even though the characteristics of each individual market may be very different. For example, the soybeans market tends to have huge bull markets that experience increasing volatility until the climatic top is reached where volatility reaches extreme levels. In addition, the soybeans market tends to have numerous weather scares in which the prices can erupt to the upside or downside with little notice. The Eurodollar market, on the other hand, tends to have smooth trends that reflect the long-term economic policies of the government. Although the Eurodollar market can at times become volatile, it tends to maintain a calm disposition when compared to the soybeans market. As we compare the Price Action Profiles of these two markets, for example, we would expect that the profiles from these significantly different markets to be very similar to the normal mound-shaped bell curve discussed in the Empirical Rule (Figure 3.7).

When we generate the Price Action Profile for each market, we will utilize all the historical data that are commonly available for each market. For each market under consideration, we generate a Price Action Profile and calculate the corresponding profile characteristics as shown in Figure 3.6. We analyze the Price Action Profiles from several futures markets obtained from different market sectors like the grains, foods, energies, metals, financial instruments, and stock indexes. Furthermore, we also analyze several Price Action Profiles from popular stocks. Analyzing a sample of vastly differing markets allows us to observe the universal effectiveness of the Value Charts and Price Action Profile concepts. Over the next several pages you will find a detailed Price Action Profile analysis for each of these different markets. After the last Price Action Profile analysis, you will find a table that compares the characteristics of all the Price Action Profiles generated from the markets in this study.

As you review the Price Action Profile analysis tables displayed on the following pages, study the characteristics of the price distributions (listed in the columns to the right of the Price Action Profiles). Observe what percentage of the Value Chart price bars fall between the ±4 and the ±8 Value Chart price levels for each different market.

As you review the Price Action Profile analysis from the Eurodollar market, for example, it is important to understand how to interpret it. The Price Action Profile is located on the left side of Figure 3.11. Using these data, we are able to determine the frequency that the Eurodollar Value Chart price bars traded within, above, and below each Value Chart price level. Note, for example, that the Eurodollars Value Chart only traded within the –1 to +1 Value Chart price range 19.19 percent of the time. This information can be seen by reviewing the

Figure 3.11 Price Action Profile from a daily Eurodollars Value Chart

Eurodollars — Daily	Price Action Profile	
	Over 12	0.18%
	Over 11	0.37%
	Over 10	0.78%
	Over 9	1.54%
	Over 8	2.99%
	Over 7	5.34%
	Over 6	8.72%
	Over 5	13.29%
	–8 to 8	94.31%
	–7 to 7	90.13%
	–6 to 6	84.06%
	–5 to 5	75.73%
	–4 to 4	65.12%
	–3 to 3	52.31%
	–2 to 2	36.83%
	–1 to 1	19.19%
	Under –5	10.68%
	Under –6	6.91%
	Under –7	4.23%
	Under –8	2.39%
	Under –9	1.24%
	Under –10	0.59%
	Under –11	0.28%
	Under –12	0.13%

| S = ±4.69 | 72% | 2S = ±9.38 | 97% | 3S = | ±14.07 |

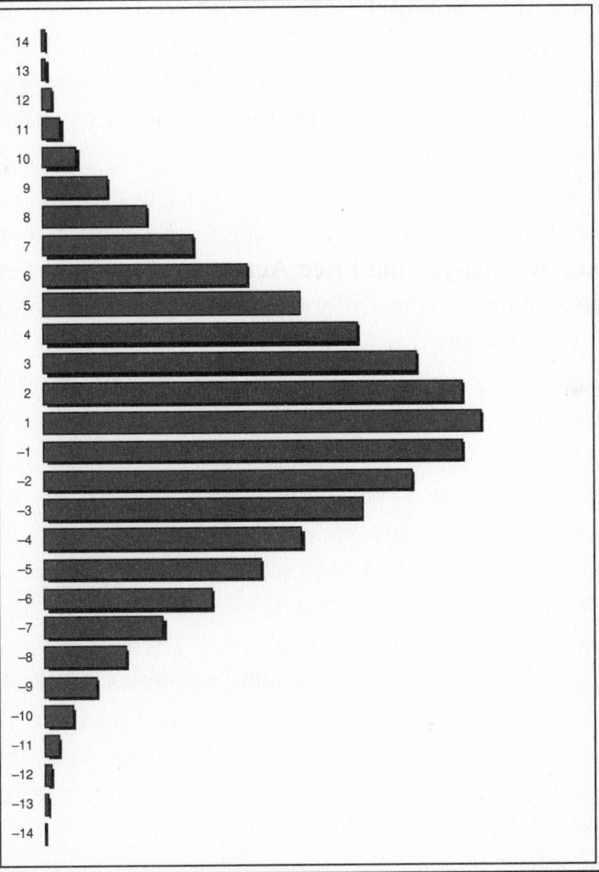

two columns on the right side of Figure 3.11. The first column identifies the range or portion of the Price Action Profile being analyzed. The second column quantifies how much Value Chart trading activity took place within, above, or below the defined range specified in the first column. Last, some Value Chart analysis indicates at the bottom of the figure how much trading activity took place within one or two standard deviations (S, 2S).

Note that ±1 standard deviation calculated from the Eurodollars Value Chart (see bottom of Figure 3.11) is equal to ±4.69 and contains 72 percent of the daily Eurodollars price bars. Furthermore, ±2 standard deviations calculated from the Eurodollars Value Chart (see bottom of Figure 3.11) is equal to ±9.38 and contains 97 percent of the daily Eurodollars price bars. Although not displayed in the figure, ±3 standard deviations calculated from the Eurodollars Value Chart is equal to ±14.07 and contains 99 percent of the daily Eurodollars price bars. The Eurodollars Price Action Profile displayed in Figure 3.11 meets the requirement of the Empirical Rule displayed in Figure 3.7 and is therefore considered a normal bell curve, which is statistically significant. Given this fact, the Eurodollars Price Action Profile allows us to make inferences about future Eurodollars price behavior.

Note that ±1 standard deviation calculated from the cocoa Value Chart (see bottom of Figure 3.12) is equal to ±4.39 and contains 69 percent of the daily cocoa price bars. Furthermore, ±2 standard deviations calculated from the cocoa Value Chart (see bottom of Figure 3.12) is equal to ±8.78 and contains 96 percent of the daily cocoa price bars. Although not displayed in the figure, ±3 standard deviations calculated from the cocoa Value Chart is equal to ±13.17 and contains 100 percent of the daily cocoa price bars. The cocoa Price Action Profile displayed in Figure 3.12 meets the requirement of the Empirical Rule displayed in Figure 3.7 and is therefore considered a normal bell curve, which is statistically significant. Given this fact, the cocoa Price Action Profile allows us to make inferences about future cocoa price behavior.

Note that ±1 standard deviation calculated from the crude oil Value Chart (see bottom of Figure 3.13) is equal to ±4.47 and contains

Figure 3.12 Price Action Profile from a daily cocoa Value Chart

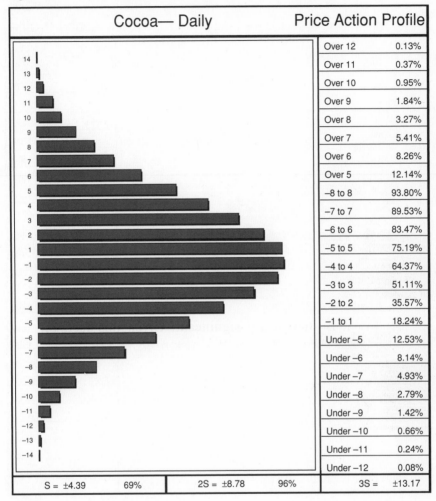

71 percent of the daily crude oil price bars. Furthermore, ±2 standard deviations calculated from the crude oil Value Chart (see bottom of Figure 3.13) is equal to ±8.94 and contains 97 percent of the daily crude oil price bars. Although not displayed in the figure, ±3 standard deviations calculated from the crude oil Value Chart is equal to ±13.41 and contains 100 percent of the daily crude oil price bars. The crude

Figure 3.13   Price Action Profile from a daily crude oil Value Chart

Crude Oil — Daily	Price Action Profile	
	Over 12	0.19%
	Over 11	0.36%
	Over 10	0.67%
	Over 9	1.28%
	Over 8	2.38%
	Over 7	4.28%
	Over 6	7.38%
	Over 5	11.90%
	−8 to 8	94.74%
	−7 to 7	91.02%
	−6 to 6	85.13%
	−5 to 5	76.75%
	−4 to 4	65.85%
	−3 to 3	52.30%
	−2 to 2	36.39%
	−1 to 1	18.67%
	Under −5	11.30%
	Under −6	7.44%
	Under −7	4.65%
	Under −8	2.83%
	Under −9	1.61%
	Under −10	0.84%
	Under −11	0.41%
	Under −12	0.16%

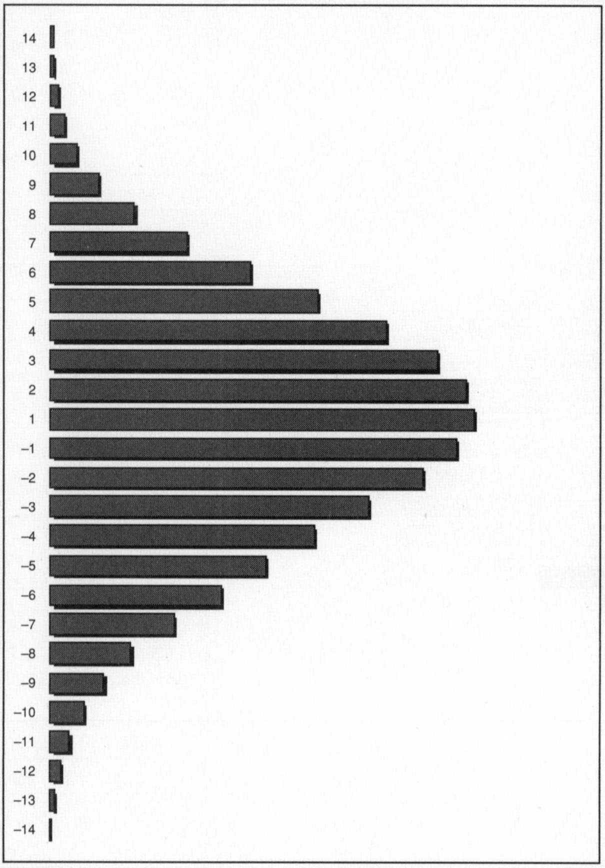

S = ±4.47	71%	2S = ±8.94	97%	3S =	±13.41

oil Price Action Profile displayed in Figure 3.13 meets the requirement of the Empirical Rule displayed in Figure 3.7 and is therefore considered a normal bell curve, which is statistically significant. Given this fact, the crude oil Price Action Profile allows us to make inferences about future crude oil price behavior.

Note that ±1 standard deviation calculated from the gold Value

Figure 3.14 Price Action Profile from a daily gold Value Chart

Gold — Daily	Price Action Profile	
	Over 12	0.22%
	Over 11	0.44%
	Over 10	0.83%
	Over 9	1.52%
	Over 8	2.59%
	Over 7	4.25%
	Over 6	6.73%
	Over 5	10.25%
	−8 to 8	94.15%
	−7 to 7	90.52%
	−6 to 6	85.19%
	−5 to 5	77.73%
	−4 to 4	67.75%
	−3 to 3	54.88%
	−2 to 2	38.97%
	−1 to 1	20.44%
	Under −5	11.95%
	Under −6	8.00%
	Under −7	5.15%
	Under −8	3.18%
	Under −9	1.85%
	Under −10	1.04%
	Under −11	0.56%
	Under −12	0.30%
S = ±4.58 74%	2S = ±9.16 97%	3S = ±13.74

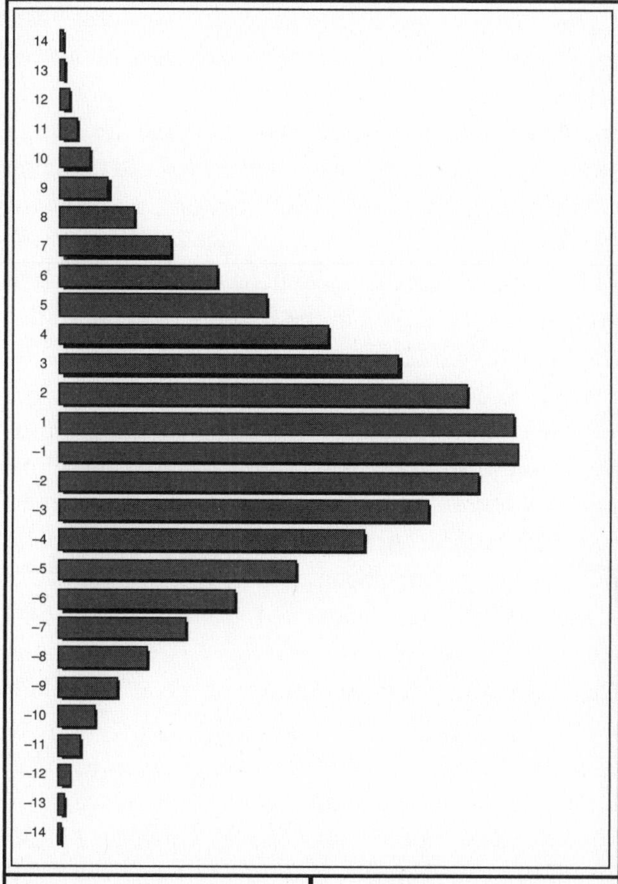

Chart (see bottom of Figure 3.14) is equal to ±4.58 and contains 74 percent of the daily gold price bars. Furthermore, ±2 standard deviations calculated from the gold Value Chart (see bottom of Figure 3.14) is equal to ±9.16 and contains 97 percent of the daily gold price bars. Although not displayed in the figure, ±3 standard deviations calculated from the gold Value Chart is equal to ±13.74 and contains 100 percent of the daily gold price bars. The gold Price Action Profile displayed in Figure 3.14 meets the requirement of the Empirical Rule displayed in Figure 3.7 and is therefore considered a normal bell curve, which is statistically significant. Given this fact, the gold Price Action Profile allows us to make inferences about future gold price behavior.

Note that ±1 standard deviation calculated from the live hogs Value Chart (see bottom of Figure 3.15) is equal to ±4.04 and contains 69 percent of the daily live hogs price bars. Furthermore, ±2 standard deviations calculated from the live hogs Value Chart (see bottom of Figure 3.15) is equal to ±8.08 and contains 96 percent of the daily live hogs price bars. Although not displayed in the figure, ±3 standard deviations calculated from the live hogs Value Chart are equal to ±12.12 and contain 100 percent of the daily live hogs price bars. The live hogs Price Action Profile displayed in Figure 3.15 meets the requirement of the Empirical Rule displayed in Figure 3.7 and is therefore considered a normal bell curve, which is statistically significant. Given this fact, the live hogs Price Action Profile allows us to make inferences about future live hogs price behavior.

Note that ±1 standard deviation calculated from the S&P 500 Value Chart (see bottom of Figure 3.16) is equal to ±4.10 and contains 71 percent of the daily S&P 500 price bars. Furthermore, ±2 standard deviations calculated from the S&P 500 Value Chart (see bottom of Figure 3.16) is equal to ±8.2 and contains 97 percent of the daily S&P 500 price bars. Although not displayed in the figure, ±3 standard deviations calculated from the S&P 500 Value Chart is equal to ±12.30 and contains 100 percent of the daily S&P 500 price bars. The S&P 500 Price Action Profile displayed in Figure 3.16 meets the requirement of the Empirical Rule displayed in Figure 3.7 and is therefore considered a normal bell curve, which is statistically significant. Given this fact, the S&P 500 Price Action Profile allows us to make inferences about future S&P 500 price behavior.

Note that ±1 standard deviation calculated from the Treasury bonds Value Chart (see bottom of Figure 3.17) is equal to ±4.22 and contains 69 percent of the daily Treasury bonds price bars. Furthermore, ±2 standard deviations calculated from the Treasury bonds

Figure 3.15 Price Action Profile from a daily live hogs Value Chart

Live Hogs — Daily	Price Action Profile	
	Over 12	0.06%
	Over 11	0.17%
	Over 10	0.46%
	Over 9	1.00%
	Over 8	2.06%
	Over 7	3.89%
	Over 6	6.87%
	Over 5	11.28%
	−8 to 8	95.75%
	−7 to 7	92.27%
	−6 to 6	86.87%
	−5 to 5	78.87%
	−4 to 4	68.03%
	−3 to 3	54.34%
	−2 to 2	38.00%
	−1 to 1	19.59%
	Under −5	9.83%
	Under −6	6.25%
	Under −7	3.82%
	Under −8	2.18%
	Under −9	1.19%
	Under −10	0.64%
	Under −11	0.31%
	Under −12	0.12%
S = ±4.04 69%	2S = ±8.08 96%	3S = ±12.12

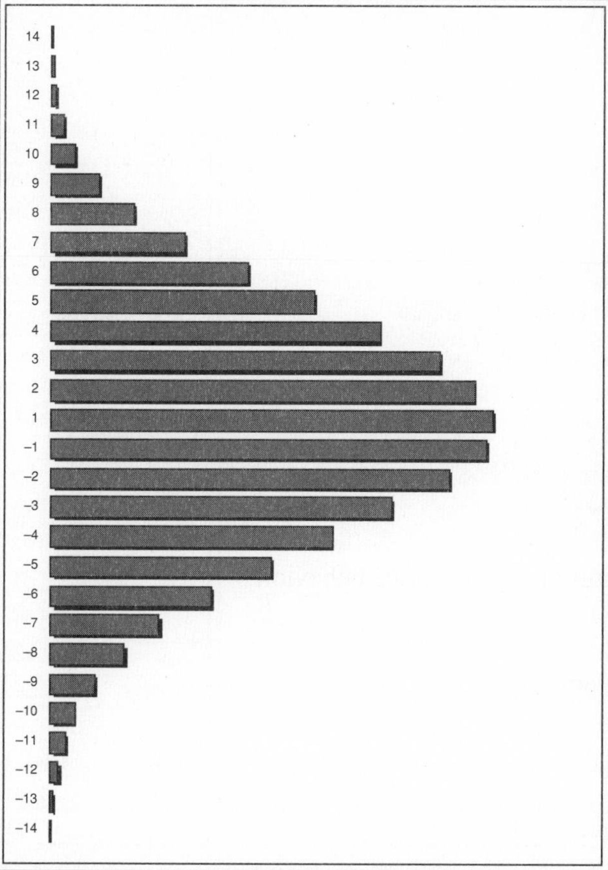

Value Chart (see bottom of Figure 3.17) is equal to ±8.44 and contains 96 percent of the daily Treasury bonds price bars. Although not displayed in the figure, ±3 standard deviations calculated from the Treasury bonds Value Chart is equal to ±12.66 and contains 100 percent of the daily Treasury bonds price bars. The Treasury bonds Price Action Profile displayed in Figure 3.17 meets the requirement of the Empiri-

Figure 3.16   Price Action Profile from a daily S&P 500 Value Chart

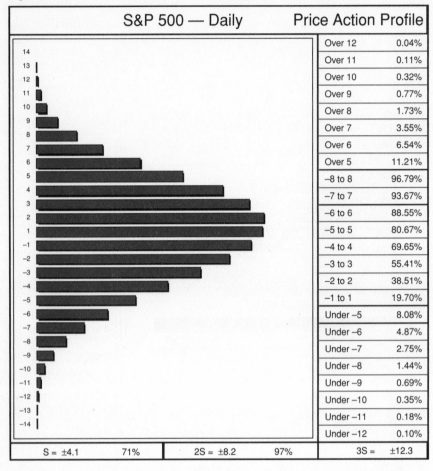

S&P 500 — Daily	Price Action Profile	
	Over 12	0.04%
	Over 11	0.11%
	Over 10	0.32%
	Over 9	0.77%
	Over 8	1.73%
	Over 7	3.55%
	Over 6	6.54%
	Over 5	11.21%
	−8 to 8	96.79%
	−7 to 7	93.67%
	−6 to 6	88.55%
	−5 to 5	80.67%
	−4 to 4	69.65%
	−3 to 3	55.41%
	−2 to 2	38.51%
	−1 to 1	19.70%
	Under −5	8.08%
	Under −6	4.87%
	Under −7	2.75%
	Under −8	1.44%
	Under −9	0.69%
	Under −10	0.35%
	Under −11	0.18%
	Under −12	0.10%

S = ±4.1	71%	2S = ±8.2	97%	3S =	±12.3

cal Rule displayed in Figure 3.7 and is therefore considered a normal bell curve, which is statistically significant. Given this fact, the Treasury bonds Price Action Profile allows us to make inferences about future Treasury bonds price behavior.

Note that ±1 standard deviation calculated from the American Express Value Chart (see bottom of Figure 3.18) is equal to ±4.17 and contains 68 percent of the daily American Express price bars. Further-

Figure 3.17 Price Action Profile from a daily Treasury bonds Value Chart

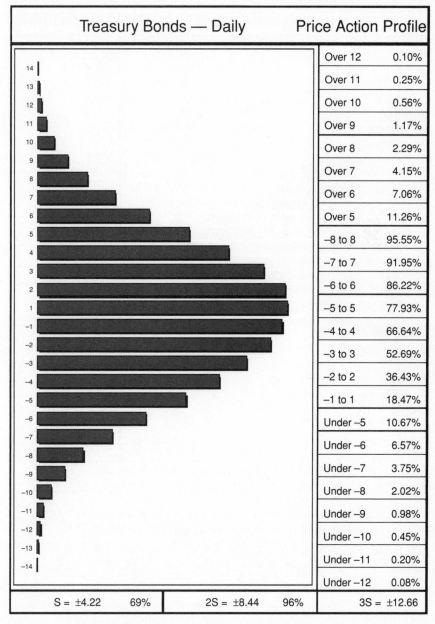

Treasury Bonds — Daily	Price Action Profile	
	Over 12	0.10%
	Over 11	0.25%
	Over 10	0.56%
	Over 9	1.17%
	Over 8	2.29%
	Over 7	4.15%
	Over 6	7.06%
	Over 5	11.26%
	−8 to 8	95.55%
	−7 to 7	91.95%
	−6 to 6	86.22%
	−5 to 5	77.93%
	−4 to 4	66.64%
	−3 to 3	52.69%
	−2 to 2	36.43%
	−1 to 1	18.47%
	Under −5	10.67%
	Under −6	6.57%
	Under −7	3.75%
	Under −8	2.02%
	Under −9	0.98%
	Under −10	0.45%
	Under −11	0.20%
	Under −12	0.08%
S = ±4.22 69%	2S = ±8.44 96%	3S = ±12.66

Figure 3.18 Price Action Profile from a daily American Express Value Chart

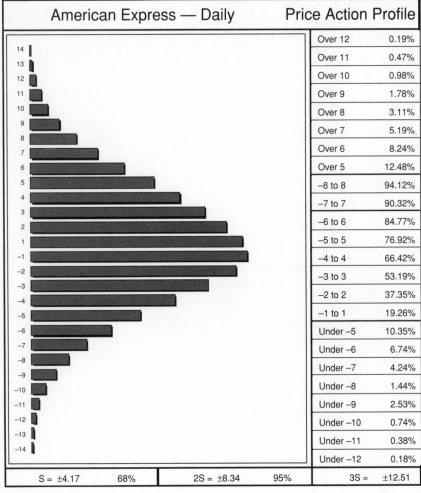

American Express — Daily	Price Action Profile	
	Over 12	0.19%
	Over 11	0.47%
	Over 10	0.98%
	Over 9	1.78%
	Over 8	3.11%
	Over 7	5.19%
	Over 6	8.24%
	Over 5	12.48%
	−8 to 8	94.12%
	−7 to 7	90.32%
	−6 to 6	84.77%
	−5 to 5	76.92%
	−4 to 4	66.42%
	−3 to 3	53.19%
	−2 to 2	37.35%
	−1 to 1	19.26%
	Under −5	10.35%
	Under −6	6.74%
	Under −7	4.24%
	Under −8	1.44%
	Under −9	2.53%
	Under −10	0.74%
	Under −11	0.38%
	Under −12	0.18%
S = ±4.17 68%	2S = ±8.34 95%	3S = ±12.51

more, ±2 standard deviations calculated from the American Express Value Chart (see bottom of Figure 3.18) is equal to ±8.34 and contains 95 percent of the daily American Express price bars. Although not displayed in the figure, ±3 standard deviations calculated from the American Express Value Chart is equal to ±12.51 and contains 99 percent of the daily American Express price bars. The American Express Price

Action Profile displayed in Figure 3.18 meets the requirement of the Empirical Rule displayed in Figure 3.7 and is therefore considered a normal bell curve, which is statistically significant. Given this fact, the American Express Price Action Profile allows us to make inferences about future American Express price behavior.

Note that ±1 standard deviation calculated from the General Motors Value Chart (see bottom of Figure 3.19) is equal to ±4.31 and

Figure 3.19   Price Action Profile from a daily General Motors Value Chart

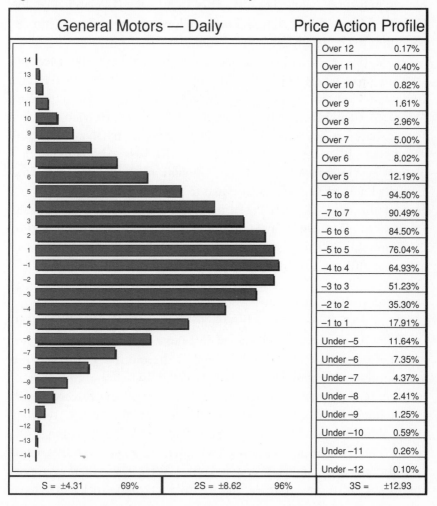

General Motors — Daily	Price Action Profile	
	Over 12	0.17%
	Over 11	0.40%
	Over 10	0.82%
	Over 9	1.61%
	Over 8	2.96%
	Over 7	5.00%
	Over 6	8.02%
	Over 5	12.19%
	−8 to 8	94.50%
	−7 to 7	90.49%
	−6 to 6	84.50%
	−5 to 5	76.04%
	−4 to 4	64.93%
	−3 to 3	51.23%
	−2 to 2	35.30%
	−1 to 1	17.91%
	Under −5	11.64%
	Under −6	7.35%
	Under −7	4.37%
	Under −8	2.41%
	Under −9	1.25%
	Under −10	0.59%
	Under −11	0.26%
	Under −12	0.10%
S = ±4.31 69%	2S = ±8.62 96%	3S = ±12.93

contains 69 percent of the daily General Motors price bars. Furthermore, ±2 standard deviations calculated from the General Motors Value Chart (see bottom of Figure 3.19) is equal to ±8.62 and contains 96 percent of the daily General Motors price bars. Although not displayed in the figure, ±3 standard deviations calculated from the General Motors Value Chart is equal to ±12.93 and contains 100 percent of the daily General Motors price bars. The General Motors Price Action Profile displayed in Figure 3.19 meets the requirement of the Empirical Rule displayed in Figure 3.7 and is therefore considered a normal bell curve, which is statistically significant. Given this fact, the General Motors Price Action Profile allows us to make inferences about future General Motors price behavior.

Note that ±1 standard deviation calculated from the Hewlett-Packard Value Chart (see bottom of Figure 3.20) is equal to ±4.18 and contains 68 percent of the daily Hewlett-Packard price bars. Furthermore, ±2 standard deviations calculated from the Hewlett-Packard Value Chart (see bottom of Figure 3.20) is equal to ±8.36 and contains 96 percent of the daily Hewlett-Packard price bars. Although not displayed in the figure, ±3 standard deviations calculated from the Hewlett-Packard Value Chart is equal to ±12.54 and contains 100 percent of the daily Hewlett-Packard price bars. The Hewlett-Packard Price Action Profile displayed in Figure 3.20 meets the requirement of the Empirical Rule displayed in Figure 3.7 and is therefore considered a normal bell curve, which is statistically significant. Given this fact, the Hewlett-Packard Price Action Profile allows us to make inferences about future Hewlett-Packard price behavior.

After reviewing Table 3.1, which represents a comparison of all the Price Action Profiles displayed in Figures 3.11 through 3.20, we are able to see that all the bell curves for these different markets are very similar. Also included in Table 3.1 is the Swiss franc currency futures market. From left to right the columns represent Soybeans (S), Eurodollar (ED), Cocoa (CC), Crude Oil (CL), Gold (GC), Live Hogs (LH), U.S. Treasury bonds (US), S&P 500 Stock Index futures (SP), Swiss franc futures day session (SF), American Express (AXP), General Motors (GM), and Hewlett-Packard (HWP). These markets represent a very diverse group of futures markets and stocks that have

Figure 3.20   Price Action Profile from a daily Hewlett-Packard Value Chart

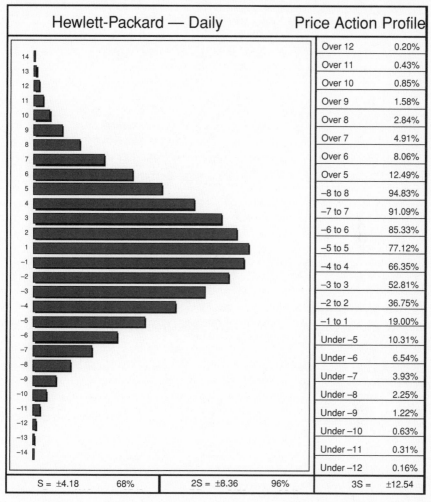

Hewlett-Packard — Daily	Price Action Profile	
	Over 12	0.20%
	Over 11	0.43%
	Over 10	0.85%
	Over 9	1.58%
	Over 8	2.84%
	Over 7	4.91%
	Over 6	8.06%
	Over 5	12.49%
	−8 to 8	94.83%
	−7 to 7	91.09%
	−6 to 6	85.33%
	−5 to 5	77.12%
	−4 to 4	66.35%
	−3 to 3	52.81%
	−2 to 2	36.75%
	−1 to 1	19.00%
	Under −5	10.31%
	Under −6	6.54%
	Under −7	3.93%
	Under −8	2.25%
	Under −9	1.22%
	Under −10	0.63%
	Under −11	0.31%
	Under −12	0.16%
S = ±4.18 68%	2S = ±8.36 96%	3S = ±12.54

significantly different characteristics. However, their Price Action Profiles are very similar. An interesting side note about Table 3.1 is that the Swiss franc futures day session (SF) Price Action Profile seems to be flatter than the other markets listed. This is important to recognize because the price activity from the Swiss franc day session does not contain or record all the trading activity for this market. A

Table 3.1 Price Action Profile analysis generated from several different markets

	S	ED	CC	CL	GC	LH	US	SP	SF	AXP	GM	HWP
Over +12	0.1%	0.2%	0.1%	0.2%	0.2%	0.1%	0.1%	0.0%	0.3%	0.2%	0.2%	0.2%
Over +11	0.3%	0.4%	0.4%	0.4%	0.4%	0.2%	0.2%	0.1%	0.7%	0.5%	0.4%	0.4%
Over +10	0.7%	0.8%	0.9%	0.7%	0.8%	0.5%	0.6%	0.3%	1.2%	1.0%	0.8%	0.9%
Over +9	1.4%	1.5%	1.8%	1.3%	1.5%	1.0%	1.2%	0.8%	2.2%	1.8%	1.6%	1.6%
Over +8	2.5%	3.0%	3.3%	2.4%	2.6%	2.1%	2.3%	1.7%	3.6%	3.1%	3.0%	2.8%
Over +7	4.3%	5.3%	5.4%	4.3%	4.2%	3.9%	4.2%	3.5%	5.7%	5.2%	5.0%	4.9%
Over +6	7.0%	8.7%	8.3%	7.4%	6.7%	6.9%	7.1%	6.5%	8.7%	8.2%	8.0%	8.1%
Over +5	10.9%	13.3%	12.1%	11.9%	10.2%	11.3%	11.3%	11.2%	12.7%	12.5%	12.2%	12.5%
-8 to +8	95.2%	94.3%	93.8%	94.7%	94.2%	95.7%	95.5%	96.8%	92.7%	94.1%	94.5%	94.8%
-7 to +7	91.7%	90.1%	89.5%	91.0%	90.5%	92.3%	92.0%	93.7%	88.2%	90.3%	90.5%	91.1%
-6 to +6	86.1%	84.1%	83.5%	85.1%	85.2%	86.9%	86.2%	88.6%	81.9%	84.8%	84.5%	85.3%
-5 to +5	77.9%	75.7%	75.2%	76.7%	77.7%	78.9%	77.9%	80.7%	73.3%	76.9%	76.0%	77.1%
-4 to +4	67.0%	65.1%	64.4%	65.8%	67.7%	68.0%	66.6%	69.7%	62.5%	66.4%	64.9%	66.4%
-3 to +3	53.3%	52.3%	51.1%	52.3%	54.9%	54.3%	52.7%	55.4%	49.6%	53.2%	51.2%	52.8%
-2 to +2	37.1%	36.8%	35.6%	36.4%	39.0%	38.0%	36.4%	38.5%	34.6%	37.3%	35.3%	36.7%
1 to +1	19.0%	19.2%	18.2%	18.7%	20.4%	19.6%	18.5%	19.7%	17.7%	19.3%	17.9%	19.0%
Under -5	11.0%	10.7%	12.5%	11.3%	11.9%	9.8%	10.7%	8.1%	13.8%	10.4%	11.6%	10.3%
Under -6	6.8%	6.9%	8.1%	7.4%	8.0%	6.2%	6.6%	4.9%	9.3%	6.7%	7.4%	6.5%
Under -7	3.9%	4.2%	4.9%	4.7%	5.2%	3.8%	3.7%	2.7%	5.9%	4.2%	4.4%	3.9%
Under -8	2.1%	2.4%	2.8%	2.8%	3.2%	2.2%	2.0%	1.4%	3.6%	2.5%	2.4%	2.2%
Under -9	1.0%	1.2%	1.4%	1.6%	1.9%	1.2%	1.0%	0.7%	2.0%	1.4%	1.2%	1.2%
Under -10	0.5%	0.6%	0.7%	0.8%	1.0%	0.6%	0.4%	0.3%	1.1%	0.7%	0.6%	0.6%
Under -11	0.2%	0.3%	0.2%	0.4%	0.6%	0.3%	0.2%	0.2%	0.5%	0.4%	0.3%	0.3%
Under -12	0.1%	0.1%	0.1%	0.2%	0.3%	0.1%	0.1%	0.1%	0.2%	0.2%	0.1%	0.2%

more accurate Price Action Profile of the Swiss franc market can be produced by using the 24-hour daily bar chart. This example underscores the importance of knowing all the details of the market that you wish to analyze.

All the Price Action Profiles generated from these different markets have very similar standard deviations. One standard deviation from the mean of a normal mound-shaped bell curve should contain approximately 68 percent of the sample data (which in this case are daily price bar data). The Price Action Profiles on average contain 69.9 percent of the daily Value Chart bars within ±1 standard deviation from zero. Furthermore, 2 standard deviations from the mean of a normal mound-shaped bell curve should contain approximately 95 percent of the sample data. The Price Action Profiles on average contain 96.3 percent of the daily Value Chart bars within ±2 standard deviations from zero. The Price Action Profile analysis displayed in Table 3.1 confirms that Value Charts are effective in adapting to significantly different market environments.

As you can see, the Price Action Profiles generated from several different markets were very similar. Recalling that the Price Action Profile simply represents the distribution of the Value Chart price activity for a market, the results displayed in Table 3.1 demonstrate that all of these markets have very similar Value Chart price distributions. Therefore, regardless of the market being analyzed, Value Charts should be effective in identifying the valuation of a market. We can now establish a convention for how we define the valuation of a market through Price Action Profiles (see Figure 3.21).

As stated above, all Value Chart prices within the ±4 Value Chart price levels will be considered fair value. This fair value range represents approximately the range ±1 standard deviation from the mean, or zero. Value Chart prices that trade between the +4 to +8 or −4 to −8 Value Chart price levels will be considered moderately overbought or moderately oversold, respectively. These moderately overbought and moderately oversold ranges represent approximately the range of Value Chart prices between ±1 standard deviation from the mean and ±2 standard deviations from the mean. Value Chart prices that trade above the +8 or below the −8 Value

Figure 3.21　Price Action Profile relative value levels

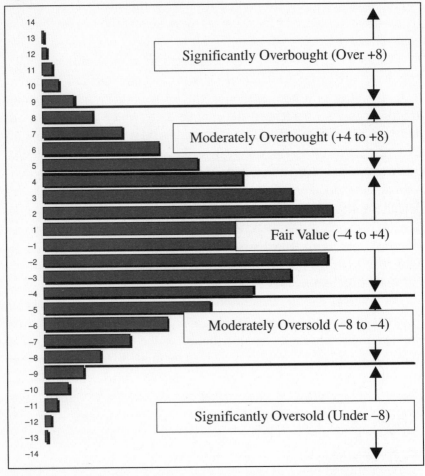

Chart price levels will be considered significantly overbought or significantly oversold, respectively. These significantly overbought and significantly oversold ranges represent approximately the range of Value Chart prices outside ±2 standard deviations from the mean, or zero. Now observe this convention on a sample value chart.

By analyzing Figures 3.22a and 3.22b, we can see that the different valuation zones are separated by four horizontal lines. The two

Figure 3.22a   Daily Treasury note price chart and Value Chart

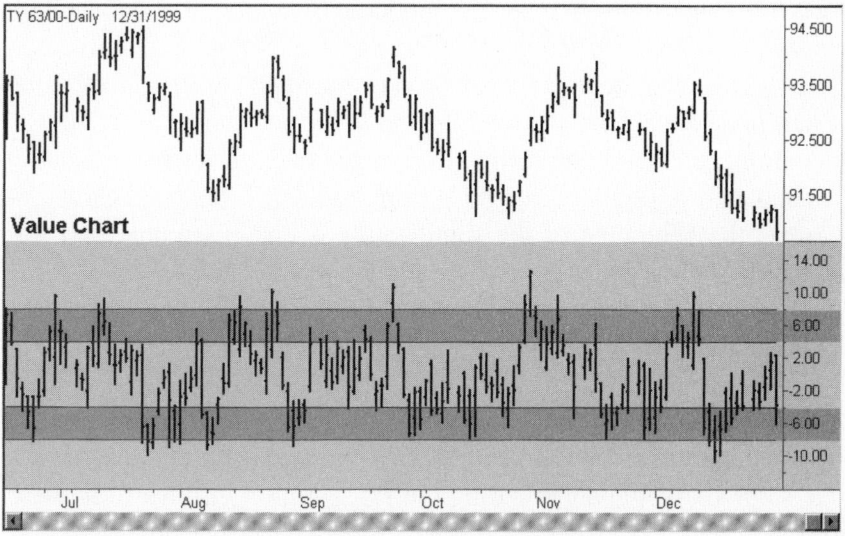

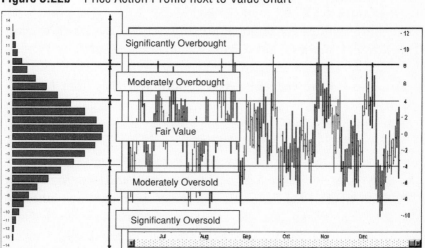

Chart created with TradeStation® 2000i by Omega Research, Inc.

Figure 3.22b   Price Action Profile next to Value Chart

Chart created with TradeStation® 2000i by Omega Research, Inc.

inner horizontal lines in the Value Chart bracket fair value. The top two horizontal lines bracket the moderately overbought (moderately overvalued) Value Chart price zone and the bottom two horizontal lines bracket the moderately oversold (moderately undervalued) Value Chart price zone. Last, the top horizontal line and above represents the beginning of the significantly overbought (significantly overvalued) Value Chart price zone, and the bottom horizontal line and below represents the beginning of the significantly oversold (significantly undervalued) price zone.

COMPARING THE PRICE ACTION PROFILES FROM TWO DIFFERENT DECADES

Another important test for the Value Charts market analysis concept will be analyzing the market activity from two different decades for the same market and comparing the Price Action Profiles from these different periods of time. Each time period will include approximately 10 years worth of daily price bar data. As you know, market volatility can significantly change from one decade to the other. During the 1980s the S&P 500 market traded around the 400 price level. During the 1990s the S&P 500 market traded around the 1,400 price level. Given the significantly different volatility characteristics from these two different decades, Value Charts should be able to effectively adapt to either decade and successfully identify the valuation of the S&P 500 futures market. The S&P 500 Price Action Profiles from these two different decades should be very similar if Value Charts effectively adapted to the continually increasing volatility in the market.

As you know, the daily volatility of the S&P 500 futures market trading around the 1,400 price level will be significantly greater than the daily volatility of the S&P 500 futures market trading around the 400 price level. If the Price Action Profiles from these two different decades are very similar, then we will conclude that the dynamic volatility units in the Value Charts are able to effectively adapt to changing volatility in the markets.

Table 3.2 displays the Price Action Profile analysis results from the S&P 500 futures market during the 1980s (SP80) and the 1990s (SP90). The analysis used to generate each column in the table utilizes

Table 3.2   Price Action Profile
comparison—S&P 500 (1980s,1990s)

	SP80	SP90
Over +12	0.0%	0.0%
Over +11	0.1%	0.1%
Over +10	0.3%	0.3%
Over +9	0.8%	0.8%
Over +8	1.8%	1.7%
Over +7	3.5%	3.6%
Over +6	6.5%	6.7%
Over +5	11.0%	11.5%
−8 to +8	96.8%	96.8%
−7 to +7	93.7%	93.6%
−6 to +6	88.5%	88.6%
−5 to +5	80.5%	80.8%
−4 to +4	69.5%	69.8%
−3 to +3	55.1%	55.6%
−2 to +2	38.2%	38.8%
−1 to +1	19.5%	19.8%
Under −5	8.6%	7.6%
Under −6	5.0%	4.7%
Under −7	2.7%	2.7%
Under −8	1.4%	1.5%
Under −9	0.7%	0.7%
Under −10	0.4%	0.3%
Under −11	0.2%	0.1%
Under −12	0.2%	0.1%

approximately 10 years of daily bar chart data. For example, the first column in Table 3.2 labeled SP80 displays the Price Action Profile analysis generated from the daily S&P 500 price bars recorded in the 1980s. The next column displays the Price Action Profile analysis generated from the daily S&P 500 price bars recorded in the 1990s. As you can see, the interval ranges (−4 to +4) and (−8 to +8) have bold dashed lines around them. This is because we have found that ±4 on the Value Chart is approximately 1 standard deviation from the mean and ±8 on the Value Chart is approximately 2 standard deviations from the mean.

As you can see in Table 3.2, it is amazing how close the Price Action Profile analysis resembles each other from the two different decades. In the 1980s, the range from –4 to +4 contained 69.5 percent of the Value Chart price activity while in the 1990s this same range contained 69.8 percent of the Value Chart price activity. Even more impressive was the fact that during the 1980s and the 1990s the range from –8 to +8 contained 96.8 percent of the Value Chart price activity. These results are very impressive given the fact that the volatility increased so dramatically during the 1990s in the S&P 500 futures market.

UNDERSTANDING PRICE ACTION PROFILE SKEW FROM TWO DIFFERENT DECADES

It is possible for the Price Action Profiles from two different decades in a given market to differ more significantly than the Price Action Profiles did from the S&P 500 example. For example, the cocoa market in the 1970s experienced an explosive decade long bull market. However, cocoa in the 1980s and the 1990s experienced a prolonged bear market (see Figure 3.23).

Figure 3.23   Monthly price chart of cocoa

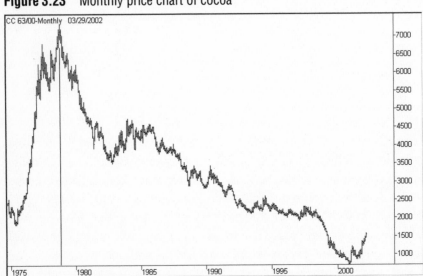

Chart created with TradeStation® 2000i by Omega Research, Inc.

We would expect the cocoa Price Action Profile from the 1970s, generated from daily cocoa Value Charts, to be skewed so that more than 50 percent of the profile would be distributed in the positive Value Chart price intervals. In the 1980s and the 1990s the profile should appear to be more normal having a slightly negative skew. Often differences in the Price Action Profiles from two different time periods can be explained by major prolonged bull or bear markets. Chapter 9 discusses the cocoa market and the advantages of utilizing conditional Price Action Profiles. When a Price Action Profile is generated from a long enough time period that is inclusive of an entire market cycle (bull and bear market), it should appear very similar to those displayed in Figures 3.11 to 3.20.

Now that we understand how Value Charts and Price Action Profiles are created, we can examine different examples of how these market analysis tools can be applied to the markets.

4

LOWERING RISK EXPOSURE

Every trade that is initiated in any free market has a level of risk exposure associated with it. For our purposes in this chapter, we define *risk exposure* as "the exposure that every trade has to the possibility of loss." Ideally, we want our trades to become profitable immediately after initiating them in the markets. Realistically, however, this is impossible to achieve. With the development of Value Charts and Price Action Profile, we are now better able to identify low risk exposure market entry points. Figure 4.1 illustrates a buying opportunity that has no risk exposure over the following 100 day time period.

Figure 4.1 illustrates a low of the day price level on July 19, 1995, that represented a buying opportunity with no risk exposure for the following 100 plus day time period. We are able to determine this by simply extending a horizontal line (as seen in Figure 4.1) from this daily low to the right (into the future) of this point, and we are able to observe that no other price bars intersect with it. The worst exposure profitability graph would never have been negative for the following 100 plus day time period (as seen in Figure 4.2).

The worst exposure profitability graph displayed in Figure 4.2 was generated by subtracting the entry buy point (low of the day from July 19, 1995) from the low of each of the following days. As

Figure 4.1 Buy point in the S&P 500 market with no risk exposure

Chart created with TradeStation® 2000i by Omega Research, Inc.

Figure 4.2 Worst exposure profitability graph generated from buy point in Figure 4.1

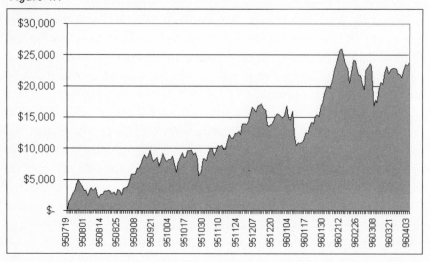

you can see, the graph has no negative values from the initiation of the trade through April 3, 1996. If we take the time to find more low risk exposure buying opportunities in Figure 4.1, we can locate sections of price bars that have no exposure to loss during the following 100 plus day time period (see Figure 4.3). These low risk exposure buying opportunities are identified with the use of a dashed horizontal line and a rectangle placed around the appropriate section of the price bar, as seen in Figure 4.3. Each labeled low risk exposure price bar section would generate a worst exposure profitability graph with no negative value over the 100 plus following days.

The same principle that defines a low risk buying opportunity would also define a low risk selling opportunity. In order for a short position to have no risk exposure to loss, we must draw a horizontal line beginning at the price under consideration and extending right toward future trading bars. Any bars trading above the horizontal line

Figure 4.3   Buy points in the S&P 500 futures market with no risk exposure

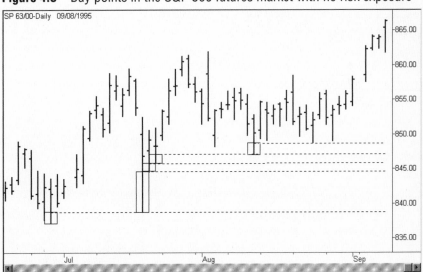

Chart created with TradeStation® 2000i by Omega Research, Inc.

would equate to risk exposure for the short position. Review Figure 4.4 and observe that the sell point under consideration had risk exposure before becoming profitable. Realistically, even when considering very good trades, we will often encounter losing periods before becoming profitable, assuming that we are correct about the near-term direction of the market. Notice that the worst exposure profitability graph, displayed in Figure 4.5, which represents the short trade in Figure 4.4, experiences negative (exposure to loss) values before becoming profitable.

The profitability graphs in Figures 4.2 and 4.5 were generated assuming one contract and no commission charges. The sum of the commission charges and the exchange fees should be subtracted from the profitability graphs for more realistic results. The profitability graphs in the preceding examples are simply provided to demonstrate how profitability is related to low exposure buying and selling opportunities. The examples of low risk exposure market entry points in Figures 4.1, 4.3, and 4.4 may seem intuitive, but the

Figure 4.4   Sell point in the gold market with low risk exposure

Chart created with TradeStation® 2000i by Omega Research, Inc.

Figure 4.5 Worst exposure profitability graph generated from sell point in Figure 4.4

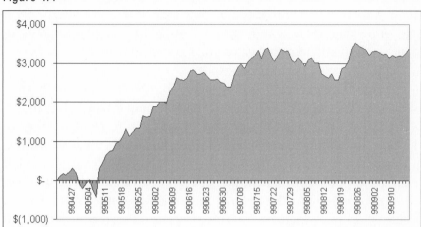

reality is that most investors do not make it a top priority to identify low risk exposure entry points in the markets. It seems that many traders overemphasize the importance of exit points for trades. However, a trader gains a tremendous advantage if he or she is able to enter into a position at low risk exposure price levels. Focusing on this aspect of trading can result in significant improvements in any trading approach.

One of the main reasons why most traders don't focus on finding low risk exposure market entry points is that there have not been any technical indicators to help identify these optimal relative price levels, until now. Value Charts and Price Action Profiles can be extremely effective tools when we are seeking to identify low risk exposure market entry points. They can be used either alone or in conjunction with other indicators or trading strategies. Value Charts and Price Action Profiles are tools that can help turn a bad trader into a good trader. They are tools that can turn a good trader into a better trader.

We can now study an example of how Value Charts and Price Action Profiles were used as a standalone market analysis strategy to identify low risk exposure buying opportunities in the S&P 500 futures market (Figure 4.6). It is important to remember that just because a market is oversold to a certain degree does not mean that it cannot become even more oversold. This is why I recommend using other effective market indicators or trading systems to complement Value Charts and Price Action Profiles.

Figure 3.16, which displays the S&P 500 Price Action Profile, shows us that the S&P 500 futures market only trades below the –6 Value Chart price level 4.87 percent of the time. Amazingly, 9 out of 17 buy opportunities are identified in Figure 4.6 that had no risk exposure for the 100 days plus following each buy signal. The other eight buy opportunities identified in Figure 4.6 experienced minimal risk exposure during the several days following the signal. The –6 Value Chart price level was selected because it seemed to work well in identifying low risk buy points at times in the past S&P 500 bull markets. It is important to note that the S&P 500 bull market exam-

Figure 4.6   Buy points identified by Value Charts with low risk exposure

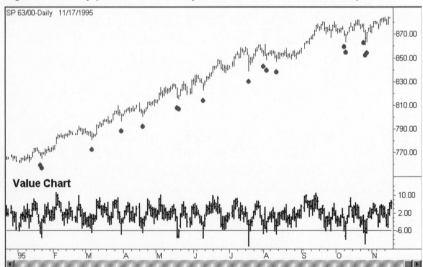

Chart created with TradeStation® 2000i by Omega Research, Inc.

ple in Figure 4.6 represented the ideal conditions for this particular trading strategy.

Now that we have demonstrated that Value Charts have the ability to identify low risk exposure market entry points, we can view the average worst exposure profitability graph (Figure 4.7) generated from all 17 buy points in Figure 4.6. Note that Value Charts allowed us identify seventeen low risk exposure buy points, as seen in the profitability graph in Figure 4.7. Although the S&P futures market was in a strong bull market during the 1995 calendar year, Value Charts was very successful in identifying the optimal buy points in this particular bull market. As you know, bull markets like the one seen in Figure 4.6 are the exception rather than the norm. For this reason, it would be prudent for traders to further enhance Value Charts and Price Action Profile with other effective indicators and trading systems.

The average worst exposure profitability graph in Figure 4.7 represents the average profitability of each of the 17 buy points from Figure 4.6 for the 100 days following each buy signal. Incredibly, within three days from the point where the S&P 500 futures market traded below the −6 Value Chart price level, the average trade was profitable.

Figure 4.7   Average worst exposure profitability graph from buy points in Figure 4.6

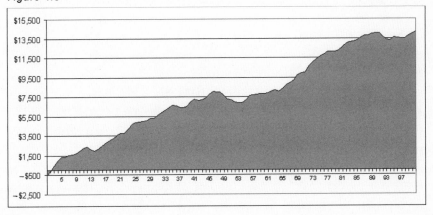

The buy signals in Figure 4.6 are as close to the perfect buy signals as one could hope to attain.

Now that we have seen several different examples of low risk market entry signals, we can review an example that compares a stock purchase with excessive risk exposure to a stock purchase with lower risk exposure. As we will learn, low risk exposure trades often become profitable sooner than higher risk exposure trades. When a trader holds a market position that is profitable, he has more flexibility with respect to his exit strategy. Most traders hate to exit a losing position because it finalizes the trade and solidifies the loss. Because of this, traders end up holding onto losing positions too long, as they hope that the losing position will turn around and eventually become profitable.

Traders need to adopt the precision of a surgeon when they are entering the market. They can do this by utilizing the power of Value Charts and Price Action Profile, either on a standalone basis or in conjunction with other indicators. We should always be on the lookout for low risk exposure market entry points. This may mean that a trader will occasionally miss out on a buying opportunity, for example, in which a market remains in an overbought state as it experiences a large directional move void of corrections. As traders, we need to align our trading expectations with the statistically likely scenario rather than the anomaly. We now consider how a normal stock purchase can be improved to reflect lower risk exposure.

Because people often want to buy into a market after it has moved up because they need price action to reinforce their opinion, they are often entering a position at short-term overbought levels. In doing this they are initiating a position that has increased exposure to risk. Assume that I am interested in buying IBM stock and buy into the market after it has increased in price, because the market has traveled in the direction that I have predicted and therefore has reinforced my opinion (see Figure 4.8).

As seen in Figure 4.8, IBM has rallied approximately $5 per share during the past five days (ending at the price bar that is farthest to the right on the chart, the current price bar). The fundamentals are looking more positive for IBM as time goes on. As we analyze the

Figure 4.8   Daily IBM price chart

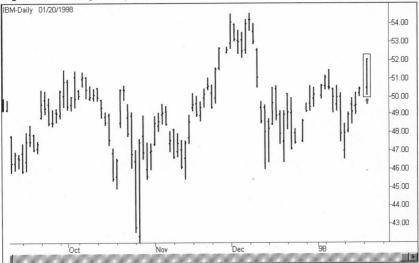

Chart created with TradeStation® 2000i by Omega Research, Inc.

chart in Figure 4.8, we get excited about the price move that could follow. However, the recent run-up of $5 has put IBM at a short term overbought level. Assume that we buy 1,000 shares of stock at the close of the day on January 20, 1998. By doing this, we are entering the market at a valuation level that contains exposure to risk. This is primarily because at this price level, IBM is short-term overvalued (see Figure 4.9).

Now that we have the capability to apply a Value Chart to the IBM daily bar chart, we are able to gain an understanding of the current market valuation on the day we are looking to buy into IBM (January 20, 1998). The closing price on January 20, 1998 is 52.02 with a Value Chart price of +9.15. From the previous chapter we learned that generally any Value Chart price over +8 or under −8 on the Value Chart is more than two standard deviations away from the mean. In other words, in general we would expect IBM to trade above the +8 Value Chart level approximately 2.5 percent of the time. What we need to do now is to analyze the Price Action Profile generated from historical IBM price activity in order to determine

Figure 4.9 Daily IBM price chart and Value Chart

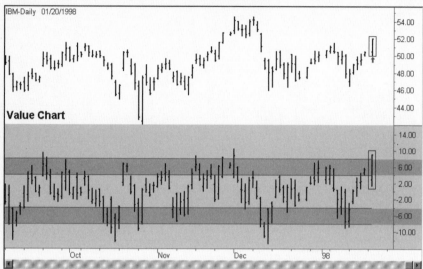

Chart created with TradeStation® 2000i by Omega Research, Inc.

how frequently the IBM Value Chart trades at each Value Chart price level (see Figure 4.10). If we do confirm that the IBM Value Chart trades above the +8 Value Chart price level very infrequently, then we can confirm that we are buying into IBM at a relative overbought price level. Buying into any market at a significantly overbought price level will most likely result in an above average exposure to risk of loss. As we stated earlier in this chapter, we need to strive for the accuracy of a surgeon and seek to enter each market at a low risk exposure price level.

By analyzing Figure 4.10, we can see that the daily IBM Value Chart trades above the +8 Value Chart price level only 2.52 percent of the time. More specifically, recall that the Value Chart closing price was +9.15. Referencing Figure 4.10, we can see that the daily IBM Value Chart trades above the +9 Value Chart price level only 1.3 percent of the time. Recall in Figures 3.21 and 3.22b that daily Value Chart price levels over +8 are considered significantly overbought on a short-term basis. We are determined to buy 1,000 shares of IBM stock because we believe that the long-term trend is going

Figure 4.10 Price Action Profile from a daily IBM Value Chart

IBM — Daily	Price Action Profile	
	Over 12	0.12%
	Over 11	0.27%
	Over 10	0.63%
	Over 9	1.30%
	Over 8	2.52%
	Over 7	4.47%
	Over 6	7.41%
	Over 5	11.58%
	−8 to 8	95.37%
	−7 to 7	91.72%
	−6 to 6	86.09%
	−5 to 5	77.94%
	−4 to 4	67.00%
	−3 to 3	53.35%
	−2 to 2	37.19%
	−1 to 1	19.08%
	Under −5	10.44%
	Under −6	6.46%
	Under −7	3.77%
	Under −8	2.07%
	Under −9	1.10%
	Under −10	0.57%
	Under −11	0.27%
	Under −12	0.12%

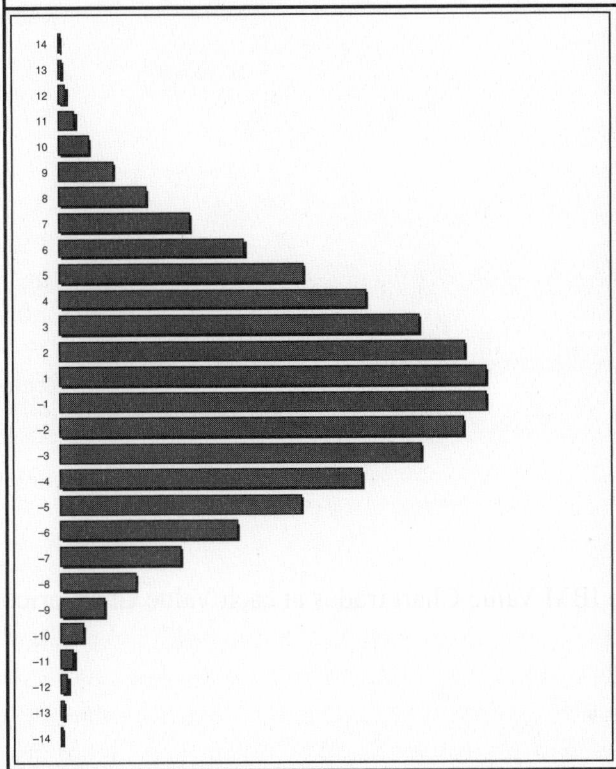

up. However, we want to enter this market at a price level that will minimize our risk exposure. Buying at a Value Chart price level of +9.15 would increase our risk exposure instead of decrease it. We therefore decide that we will enter IBM at a Value Chart price level of −5 because the IBM Value Chart only trades below this level 10.44 percent of the time. Now we will determine if our decision to buy IBM at a more prudent Value Chart price level will pay off by examining the price activity of IBM on the days following January 20, 1998 (Figure 4.11).

Note that in Figure 4.11 IBM sold off sharply during the days following our initial target market entry date. In fact, IBM opened

Figure 4.11   Daily IBM price chart and Value Chart

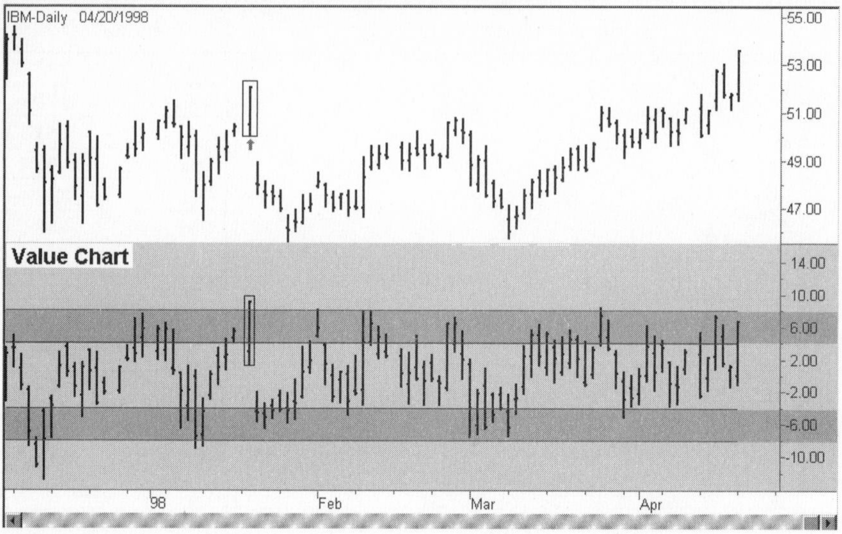

Chart created with TradeStation® 2000i by Omega Research, Inc.

up at $47.98 the next morning, equating to a Value Chart open of
–4.49. The low of the day ended up trading below our target Value
Chart price level of –5. This enabled us to buy 1,000 shares of IBM
at $47.79 per share. Because we waited to buy IBM at a moderately
undervalued Value Chart price level (under –5) instead of buying
the previous day when IBM closed at $52.02 (+9.15 Value Chart
price level), we were able to significantly decrease our risk exposure. The risk exposure of buying IBM at a Value Chart price level
of +9.15 (which is significantly overbought on a short-term relative
basis) has become apparent on the following day as we see that
IBM opened up $4.04 a share lower than the previous day's close.
If we had bought IBM at $52.02, we would have incurred a loss
right from the start of our trade because IBM sold off the following
day, as seen in Figure 4.11. We saved $4,230.00 on the price of the
1,000 shares of IBM stock because we were able to utilize the
power of Value Charts and effectively identify relative overbought
and oversold price levels.

Now let us further analyze the profitability of these two different scenarios that were discussed in the preceding paragraph. In the first scenario we purchased 1,000 shares of IBM at $52.02 a share (significantly overbought) and in the second scenario we purchased 1,000 shares of IBM at $47.79 a share (moderately oversold), as indicated by the Value Chart. We can now look at profitably charts for these two scenarios in Figures 4.12a, 4.12b, and 4.12c.

The profitability charts in Figures 4.12a, 4.12b, and 4.12c were generated by calculating the profit or loss (as determined by the closing prices of IBM on the days following market entry) generated from buying 1,000 shares of IBM stock in each of the two scenarios that we considered. Examine Figure 4.12a, where we find a profitability chart in which we bought IBM at $52.02 per share (which equates to a +9.15 Value Chart price level). In this example we have waited for the price of IBM to rally, and hence reinforce our bullish opinion on the market. Unfortunately, by requiring this positive reinforcement, we are entering the stock at a significantly overbought price level.

In Figure 4.12b, we see the profitability chart in which we bought IBM at $47.79 per share (which equates to a −5.00 Value Chart price level). In this scenario we also are bullish on IBM, but in this case we

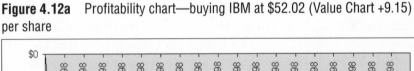

Figure 4.12a Profitability chart—buying IBM at $52.02 (Value Chart +9.15) per share

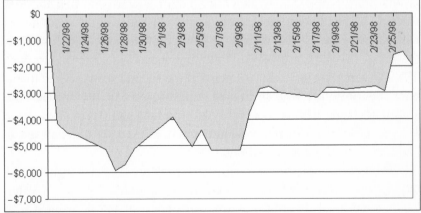

Figure 4.12b Profitability chart—buying IBM at $47.79 (Value Chart –5.00) per share

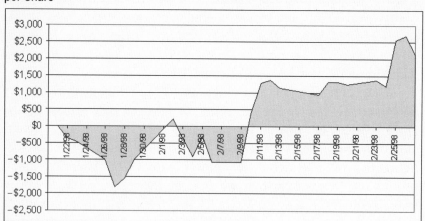

strategically enter into our IBM stock position by utilizing the power of Value Charts and Price Action Profile to help identify overbought and oversold price levels in the market. As we analyze each scenario and compare them (as seen in Figure 4.12c), we find that the second strategy has greatly reduced our risk exposure.

After 27 days have passed by, we see that the trade in the first scenario (buying IBM at $52.02) is still losing $1,969 while the trade in the second scenario (buying IBM at $47.79) has realized $2,199 in profits. Furthermore, after analyzing both cases we see that the first scenario had to endure greater exposure to losses than the second scenario. During the 27-day period the worst drawdown (equity loss from the initial investment level) that the first scenario had to endure was –$5,937 while the worst drawdown that the second scenario had to endure was only –$1,769. In this example we can clearly see that the ability of Value Charts to identify overbought and oversold relative price levels can reduce our exposure to risk as we enter into any stock, bond, or futures market positions.

Another example that we will study compares the risk exposure of buying into a bull market in American Express either at the +8 Value Chart price level or buying it when it trades at the –8 Value Chart

Figure 4.12c Buying 1,000 shares IBM at $52.02 vs. $47.79 per share

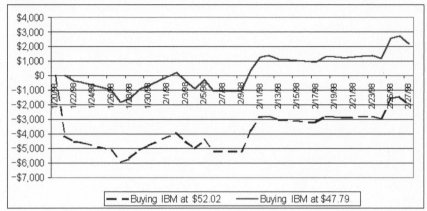

price level. When an investment or trade has a low exposure to risk, it typically has a greater chance to realize profits. We will now analyze a bull market in American Express (as seen in Figure 4.13). Bull markets are generally good environments for traders looking to buy. When traders are looking to buy, or go long, in a bull market, then their chances of making money should be good.

After viewing the American Express price chart in Figure 4.13, it is evident that anyone looking to buy shares of this stock during this time period should make money. Conventional wisdom encourages traders to trade in the same direction of the trend. As we discuss in the previous example, many people buy into a market after it has rallied because it reinforces their market opinion. However, we can also look at another scenario where we seek to identify strategic entry points with low risk exposure in the strong bull market in American Express.

We need to generate a Value Chart for the American Express daily bar chart displayed in Figure 4.13. However, we will first create and review a Price Action Profile analysis of the historical American Express daily Value Chart activity (Figure 4.14).

As you can see in Figure 4.14, the Price Action Profile of the American Express historical Value Chart price activity resembles a mound-shaped bell curve. Utilizing the Price Action Profile analysis

Figure 4.13   Daily American Express price chart

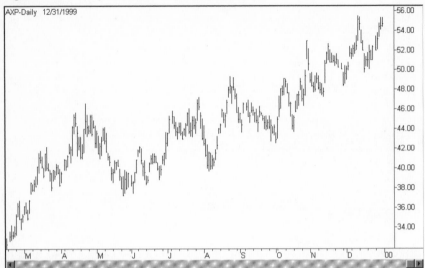

Chart created with TradeStation® 2000i by Omega Research, Inc.

in Figure 4.14, we can look to identify low risk exposure price levels to buy shares of American Express in the strong bull market that is displayed in Figure 4.13. We will look for buying opportunities when the American Express Value Chart trades below the –8 Value Chart price level. By utilizing the Price Action Profile analysis in Figure 4.14, we can see that the American Express Value Chart only trades below the –8 Value Chart price level 2.53 percent of the time. We will now generate a Value Chart of the American Express bar chart displayed in Figure 4.13 (see Figure 4.15).

When we review Figure 4.15, we can see that many of the points at which the Value Chart dips below the –8 Value Chart price level coincide with reduced risk exposure buying opportunities. Ideally, when we buy or sell into any market, we would like to be profitable from the inception of our trade. However, in the real world we often have to endure losing money on a trade before the trade has the opportunity to become profitable, assuming that it eventually will. When we analyze the short-term price behavior of most markets, we observe that price tends to oscillate between

Figure 4.14   Price Action Profile from a daily American Express Value Chart

American Express — Daily	Price Action Profile	
	Over 12	0.19%
	Over 11	0.47%
	Over 10	0.98%
	Over 9	1.78%
	Over 8	3.11%
	Over 7	5.19%
	Over 6	8.24%
	Over 5	12.48%
	−8 to 8	94.12%
	−7 to 7	90.32%
	−6 to 6	84.77%
	−5 to 5	76.92%
	−4 to 4	66.42%
	−3 to 3	53.19%
	−2 to 2	37.35%
	−1 to 1	19.26%
	Under −5	10.35%
	Under −6	6.74%
	Under −7	4.24%
	Under −8	2.53%
	Under −9	1.41%
	Under −10	0.74%
	Under −11	0.38%
	Under −12	0.18%

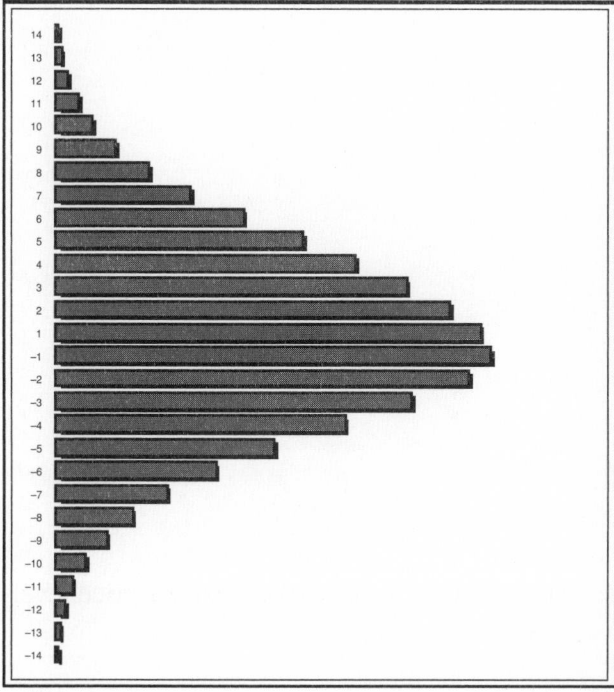

overvalued price levels and undervalued price levels. As market volatility increases, this oscillation increases. Before Value Charts, it was very difficult to define the relative valuation in constantly changing markets. Now, however, Value Charts enable us to better locate market entry points that have reduced exposure to risk of loss. The ability to enter markets with a reduced exposure to the risk of loss can significantly improve a trader's chances of generating profits.

We will now take a closer look at the American Express price bars that dipped below the −8 Value Chart price level in Figure 4.15. We will identify these price bars by putting a dot below them (see Figure 4.16).

We can see from Figure 4.16 that many of the price bars that

Figure 4.15 Daily American Express price chart and Value Chart

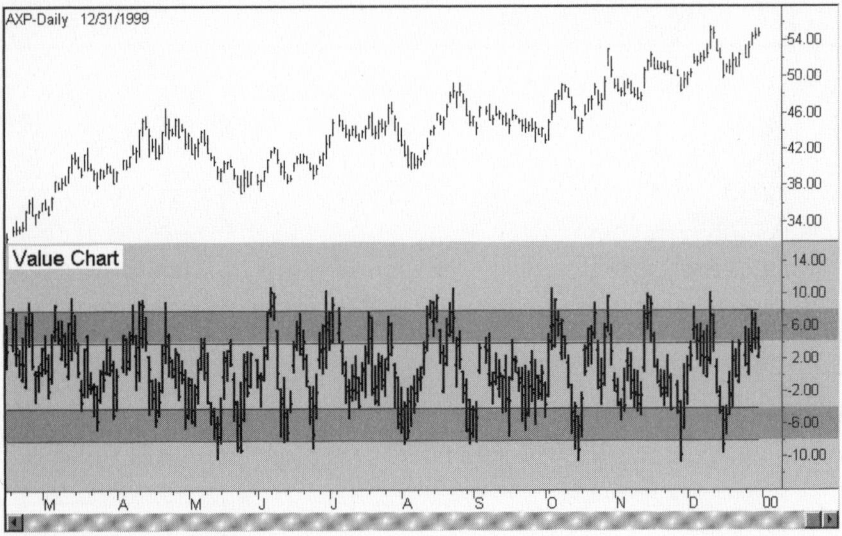

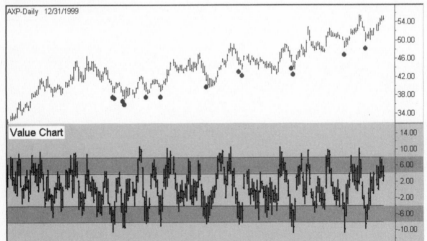

Chart created with TradeStation® 2000i by Omega Research, Inc.

Figure 4.16 Low risk exposure buying points on daily American Express price chart

Chart created with TradeStation® 2000i by Omega Research, Inc.

dipped below the –8 Value Chart price level coincided with good buying opportunities. In Figure 4.17 we can see the American Express Value Chart price bars that exceeded the +8 Value Chart price level, also labeled with dots.

The chart in Figure 4.18 displays the average profit (loss) of all the market entry data points displayed in both Figures 4.16 and 4.17. All 13 of the buy signals displayed in Figure 4.16, which bought into American Express at the –8 Value Chart price level, were averaged together to produce the solid profitability line (top) in Figure 4.18. All 28 of the buy signals displayed in Figure 4.17, which bought into American Express at the +8 Value Chart price level, were averaged together to produce the dashed line (bottom) in Figure 4.18.

After a buy signal was generated in Figure 4.16, we determined the profit or loss on the trade by subtracting the entry price from the closing prices of the following 10 days. By viewing the chart in Figure

Figure 4.17   Higher risk exposure buying points on daily American Express price chart

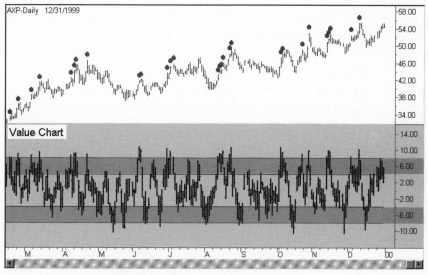

Chart created with TradeStation® 2000i by Omega Research, Inc.

Figure 4.18   Average profitability from buying American Express at –8 vs. +8

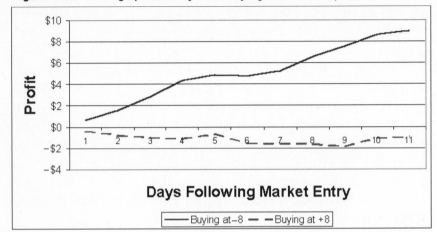

4.18, we can see that the average profitability from the 13 buy signals in Figure 4.16 on the eleventh day of these trades was $8.94. On the other hand, the average profitability from the 28 buy signals in Figure 4.17 on the eleventh day of these trades was –$0.91. We can clearly see that the average profitability for the 11 day time period following each of the 2 different market entry scenarios demonstrated the advantages of using the strategy that bought at significantly oversold price levels. On average, buying into the American Express bull market at the –8 Value Chart price level reduced our risk exposure.

We can take a closer look at the first eight buy signals in Figure 4.17 (as seen in Figure 4.19). As you can see, without Value Charts none of these buy entries would seem like unreasonable places to enter American Express. However, on average, even in a strong bull market, Figure 4.18 proves that Value Charts and Price Action Profile are effective tools in identifying significantly overbought (higher risk exposure buy signals) and significantly oversold (lower risk exposure buy signals).

Now we can see how amazing several of the lower risk exposure buy points were from Figure 4.16 (see Figure 4.20).

In order to fully appreciate the low risk exposure buying

Figure 4.19   First eight higher risk exposure buy points on daily American Express price chart from Figure 4.17

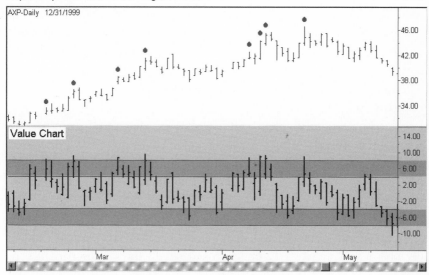

Chart created with TradeStation® 2000i by Omega Research, Inc.

Figure 4.20   First six low risk exposure buy points on daily American Express price chart from Figure 4.16

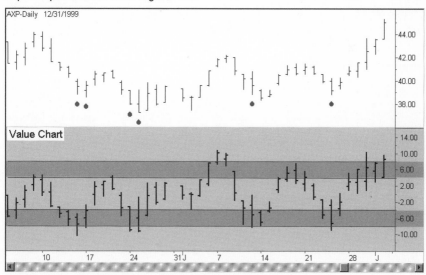

Chart created with TradeStation® 2000i by Omega Research, Inc.

opportunities as displayed in Figure 4.20, we need to understand that we would consider only buying the portions of the tagged price bars (as identified by a dot placed under them) that penetrated below the –8 Value Chart price level (which is identified by the lowest of the four lines on the Value Chart). By analyzing the last of the six tagged price bars in Figure 4.17, we can fully appreciate just how low the risk of loss is in some of these buying opportunities (see Figure 4.21).

The buy signal displayed in Figure 4.21, generated from trading activity that penetrated below the –8 Value Chart price level, included the bottom $0.50 portion of the American Express price bar on June 24, 1999. The maximum exposure to loss was a $0.17 short-lived losing period between the entry level ($39.00) on June 24, 1999, and the low of the same trading day ($38.83). This position became immediately profitable after the signal day and soon rose 16 percent ($6.26) per share as American Express closed seven days later (on July 6,

Figure 4.21   Last low risk exposure buy point on daily American Express price chart from Figure 4.20. Buy signal is boxed portion of price bar

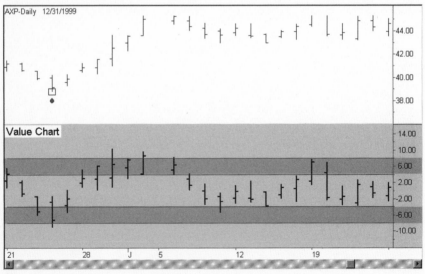

Chart created with TradeStation® 2000i by Omega Research, Inc.

1999) at a price level of $45.26. Although the trading signal displayed in Figure 4.21 was an ideal scenario, it nevertheless exemplified the potential of Value Charts and Price Action Profile as market analysis tools.

Realistically, Value Charts and Price Action Profile should become just one key component of a trading approach. In other words, many other technical and fundamental trading tools can be used in conjunction with Value Charts and Price Action Profile in order to increase the effectiveness of an overall trading approach.

5

ENHANCING VALUE CHARTS
WITH SHORT-TERM TRADING SYSTEMS

In Chapter 4 we learned that Value Charts and Price Action Profile can be valuable market analysis tools for reducing risk exposure. We now know that attaining lower short-term risk exposure should be an important consideration for every market participant. Conventional wisdom tells us that no market analysis tool is perfect, and Value Charts and Price Action Profile are no exception. However, we can often improve our overall trading strategy by utilizing Value Charts and Price Action Profile in conjunction with other technical indicators or trading systems. Consider the recent bull market in crude oil (as seen in Figure 5.1). It is important to note that the crude oil chart in Figure 5.1, along with others in this book, were constructed as continuous forward-adjusted charts. Because of this, the y-axis point values are not accurate even though the price activity of the crude oil market is accurate.

Notice in Figure 5.1 that Value Charts and Price Action Profile successfully identified six short-term bottoms in the crude oil bull market by flagging the Value Chart price bars that traded below the −8 Value Chart price level. Upon reviewing the Price Action Profile analysis of crude oil in Figure 5.2, we can see that the crude oil market only trades below the −8 Value Chart price level 2.83 percent of the time. We also notice (in Figure 5.1) that in October the crude oil mar-

Figure 5.1   Low risk exposure buying points on daily crude oil price chart

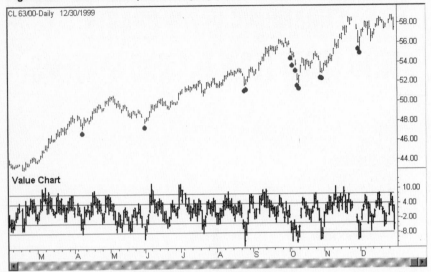

Chart created with TradeStation® 2000i by Omega Research, Inc.

ket experienced a more significant correction that ended up exceeding the first three flagged price bars. If we had simply entered into a long position when the Value Chart first penetrated below the −8 level during this more significant correction, using only Value Charts and the Price Action Profile as our guides, we would have been exposed to a loss on our position during the first several days of our trade.

COMPLEMENTING VALUE CHARTS WITH A SHORT-TERM TRADING SYSTEM

Although we were able to identify six ideal buying opportunities in Figure 5.1 by flagging any price bars that traded below the −8 Value Chart price level, we had one instance when the crude oil market experienced an unusually large correction in October 1999. Therefore, we flagged five consecutive crude oil price bars because the crude oil Value Chart traded below the −8 Value Chart price level for five consecutive days. If we had simply bought into crude oil anytime it traded below the −8 Value Chart price level in Figure 5.1 (as indicated by the flagged price bars), we would have participated in 10 low exposure

Figure 5.2   Price Action Profile from a daily crude oil Value Chart

Crude Oil — Daily	Price Action Profile	
	Over 12	0.19%
	Over 11	0.36%
	Over 10	0.67%
	Over 9	1.28%
	Over 8	2.38%
	Over 7	4.28%
	Over 6	7.38%
	Over 5	11.90%
	−8 to 8	94.74%
	−7 to 7	91.02%
	−6 to 6	85.13%
	−5 to 5	76.75%
	−4 to 4	65.85%
	−3 to 3	52.30%
	−2 to 2	36.39%
	−1 to 1	18.67%
	Under −5	11.30%
	Under −6	7.44%
	Under −7	4.65%
	Under −8	2.83%
	Under −9	1.61%
	Under −10	0.84%
	Under −11	0.41%
	Under −12	0.16%

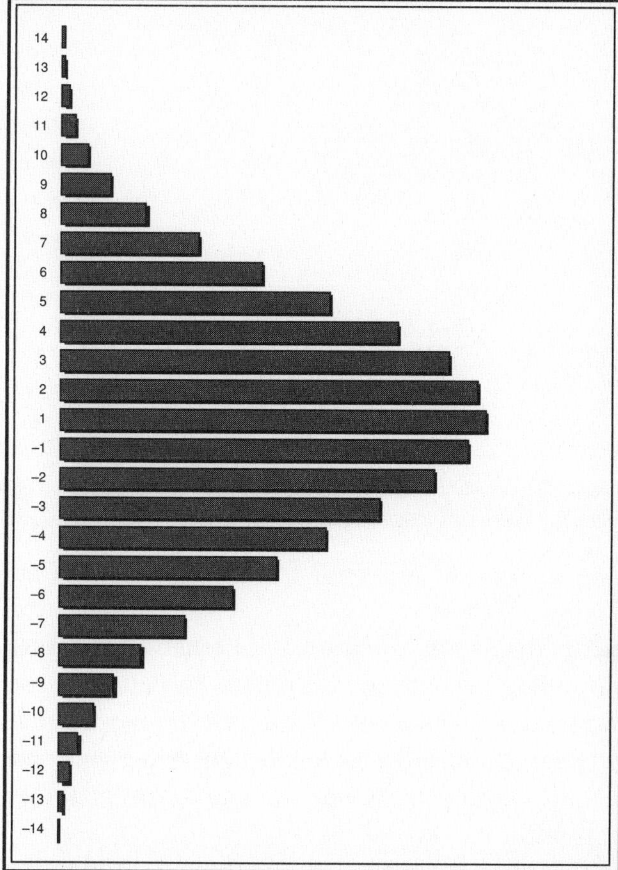

buying opportunities (10 flagged bars identifying 6 crude oil corrections) and 3 higher exposure buying opportunities (identified by the box in Figure 5.3).

Notice that in Figure 5.3 the three price bars, identified by the dots beneath them, in the box met the requirement of having traded below the −8 Value Chart price level. However, as we can see, these price bars were not low risk buying opportunities like the other

Figure 5.3 False signal low risk exposure buying points on daily crude oil price chart

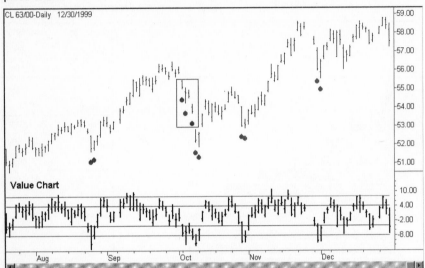

Chart created with TradeStation® 2000i by Omega Research, Inc.

eight flagged price bars displayed in Figure 5.3. Perhaps if we were to add a short-term trading system to a 30-minute bar chart of the crude oil market, we could enhance our overall effectiveness in entering the crude oil market during corrections. In doing this, we would hopefully avoid entering the crude oil market prematurely during larger corrections.

One could simply apply a basic breakout trading program to the 30-minute bar chart of the crude oil market and follow only the trading signals if certain rules were satisfied. Listed in Figure 5.4 are the rules for applying a short-term trading system to the 30-minute bar chart of crude oil in the hope of increasing the effectiveness of Value Charts and Price Action Profile in identifying low risk market entry points.

The trading rules as stated in Figure 5.4 simply state that we will buy crude oil when (1) an uptrend has been established, (2) crude oil trades below the −8 Value Chart price level, and (3) a buy signal is

Figure 5.4   Crude oil trading strategy rules

Buy Signal

Buy highest (high,10) + 1 point stop (applied to a 30-minute crude oil bar chart).

ExitLong Signal

Exitlong at +8 Value Chart price level or higher (applied to a daily crude oil value chart).

Money Management Stop

Place money-management stop 1 tick below lowest low in 30-minute bar chart for the 10 bars preceding the short-term breakout system buy signal.

Crude Oil Buy Strategy

Filter One   Uptrend will be established by a trend-following system. Only follow trading signals in the direction of the trend. When a 25-day simple moving average of the closing prices crosses above (and remains above) a 75-day simple moving average of the closing prices, then an uptrend will be indicated.

Filter Two (Buy Signal)   Once an uptrend is indicated by the moving average trend-following system (Filter One), look to buy into the crude oil market when it trades below the –8 Value Chart price level. As we can see in Figure 5.2, which displays the crude oil Price Action Profile analysis, crude oil only trades below the –8 Value Chart price level 2.83 percent of the time.

Short-Term Trading System to Enhance Value Charts   If the two previous filters are satisfied, we will use a 10-bar breakout system applied to a 30-minute bar chart to generate our buy signals. This short-term system will be turned on once the crude oil market trades below the –8 Value Chart price level and crude oil is in an uptrend, as defined by Filter One. Once the short-term breakout trading system is turned on, we will take the next buy signal. All other subsequent buy signals (generated from the 10-bar breakout system) will be ignored, and all sell signals (generated from the 10-bar breakout system) will be ignored.

generated by a 10-bar breakout system applied to 30-minute bar charts. We will exit our long position when the crude oil Value Chart trades above the +8 Value Chart price level or gets stopped out below our 30-minute bar chart entry point.

The purpose of reviewing this example trading system is simply to demonstrate how many different trading tools (systems) can be used to enhance Value Charts and Price Action Profile. Our goal is to identify low risk market entry points. If we are able to enter a market at a low risk price level, we have much more flexibility in determining how to exit our position. If we enter a market at a high risk exposure price level, we most likely will experience a loss during the first several days of our trade, even if we are right about the direction of the long-term trend. The potential applications of Value Charts and Price Action Profile in the field of trading system development are numerous. We can now continue to evaluate our example trading strategy (Figure 5.4) as applied to the crude oil bull market in 1999. Our first step is to confirm that crude oil is in a bull market as defined by Filter One listed in Figure 5.4. We can view a chart to confirm that this market is indeed in an uptrend as defined by the moving average crossover trading system (see Figure 5.5).

As you can see in Figure 5.5, the moving average trend-following system went long crude oil on March 8, 1999, and remained long through the end of the calendar year. Therefore the trend-following system (Filter One in Figure 5.4) indicates an uptrend.

Recall that in Figure 5.1 we observed the daily crude oil price bars that traded below the –8 Value Chart price level, as indicated by the dots. These price bars meet the requirements of the second filter in Figure 5.4. Note that there are a total of 13 flagged price bars that identify 6 crude oil price corrections. We can now evaluate the short-term trading system buy signals. As you know from Figure 5.4, the breakout trading system buy signals will be considered only when the crude oil market is in an uptrend and, at the same time, is trading below the –8 Value Chart price level. Starting with Figure 5.6, each of the 6 crude oil corrections will be displayed along with the corresponding short-term trading signals generated from the breakout trading system. Again, the y-axis point values on the right side of the bar

Figure 5.5   Trend-following moving average system applied to daily crude oil price chart

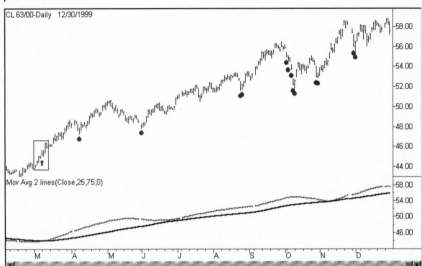

Chart created with TradeStation® 2000i by Omega Research, Inc.

charts are not important because the continuous price activity plotted on the charts is accurate.

We can review the results from the trades displayed in Figures 5.6 through 5.17. All of these trades were generated from the trading rules outlined in Figure 5.4. It is important to note that the daily charts displayed in Figures 5.6, 5.8, 5.10, 5.12, 5.14, and 5.16 are continuous forward-adjusted crude oil price charts. The contract rollover gaps have been removed resulting in an accurate representation of the *y*-axis price labels. However, the crude oil price movement is accurate and the analysis is sound. Likewise, the 30-minute crude oil price charts displayed in Figures 5.7, 5.9, 5.11, 5.13, 5.15, and 5.17 are also continuous forward-adjusted crude oil price charts. When we are testing any trading system on any futures markets, it is important to construct continuous forward-adjusted or continuous back-adjusted charts. This will insure that the resulting profits or losses generated from your testing will be representative of the contract price movement and not the rollover price gaps. Displayed in

Figure 5.6   Low risk exposure buying point on April 8,1999

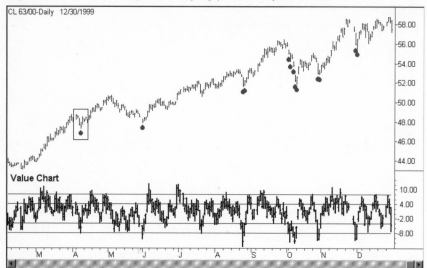

Chart created with TradeStation® 2000i by Omega Research, Inc.

Table 5.1 are the trading results from the trades covered in Figure 5.6 through Figure 5.17.

The trading system results displayed in Table 5.1 are encouraging. When we were calculating the trading results, a $25 per round turn commission was applied to each trade. Furthermore, it was assumed each trade bought and sold one crude oil contract, and also it was assumed that the slippage was insignificant.

The crude oil buy trading system (Figure 5.4) was successful in realizing profits in the crude oil market in 1999. The average winning trade was more than twice the size of the average losing trade. The average risk per trade, assuming that the crude oil market didn't gap through our money management stops, was $535 per trade. Note that on October 7, 1999, the crude oil market did indeed gap through our stop as is evident from the fact that the loss realized from this trade was larger than our predetermined risk, which was established by our money management stop. The percentage of winning trades was impressive at 75 percent.

The purpose of applying the trading strategy displayed in Figure 5.4

Table 5.1 Trading results from the crude oil buy strategy (Figure 5.4)

Reference Charts	Entry Date	Buy Price ($ per barrel)	Exit Date	Exit/long Price ($ per barrel)	Profit/Loss ($)	Risk (Stop) ($)
Figure 5.6,7	April 9, 1999	15.33	April 16, 1999	16.47	$1,115.00	$635.00
Figure 5.8,9	June 2, 1999	15.61	June 4, 1999	16.49	$855.00	$255.00
Figure 5.10,11	August 26, 1999	19.29	September 9, 1999	21.68	$2,365.00	$375.00
Figure 5.12,13	October 6, 1999	22.56	October 7, 1999	21.58	$(1,005.00)	$755.00
Figure 5.12,13	October 11, 1999	20.21	October 25, 1999	22.76	$2,525.00	$635.00
Figure 5.14,15	October 29, 1999	21.14	October 29, 1999	20.58	$(585.00)	$535.00
Figure 5.14,15	November 1, 1999	21.06	November 10, 1999	23.55	$2,465.00	$535.00
Figure 5.16,17	December 1, 1999	24.20	November 11, 1999	26.58	$2,355.00	$555.00

Total Profit/Loss	$10,090.00
Average Winning Trade	$1,946.67
Average Losing Trade	$(795.00)
Average Risk per Trade	$535.00
Percent Winning Trades	75%

Figure 5.7   Short-term breakout system buy signal on April 9, 1999

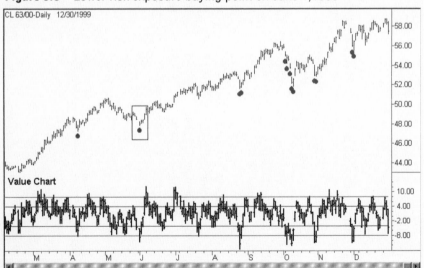

Chart created with TradeStation® 2000i by Omega Research, Inc.

Figure 5.8   Lower risk exposure buying point on June 1, 1999

Chart created with TradeStation® 2000i by Omega Research, Inc.

Figure 5.9   Short-term breakout system buy signal on June 2,1999

Chart created with TradeStation® 2000i by Omega Research, Inc.

Figure 5.10   Lower risk exposure buying points on August 25–26,1999

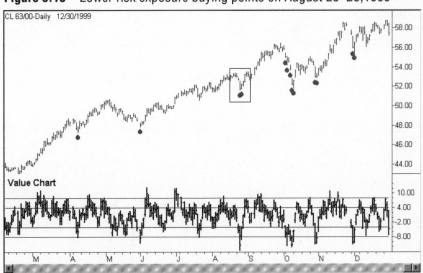

Chart created with TradeStation® 2000i by Omega Research, Inc.

Figure 5.11 Short-term breakout system buy signal on August 26, 1999

Chart created with TradeStation® 2000i by Omega Research, Inc.

Figure 5.12 Lower risk exposure buying points on October 4–11, 1999

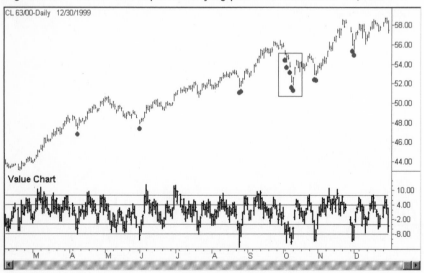

Chart created with TradeStation® 2000i by Omega Research, Inc.

Figure 5.13 Short-term breakout system buy signals on October 6 and 11, 1999

Chart created with TradeStation® 2000i by Omega Research, Inc.

Figure 5.14 Low risk exposure buying points on October 28–29,1999

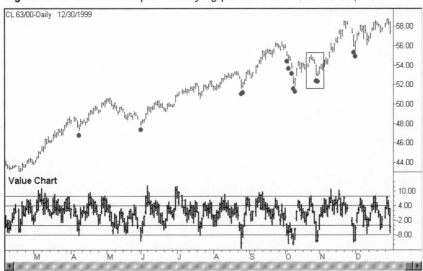

Chart created with TradeStation® 2000i by Omega Research, Inc.

Figure 5.15 Short-term breakout system buy signals on October 29–November 1, 1999

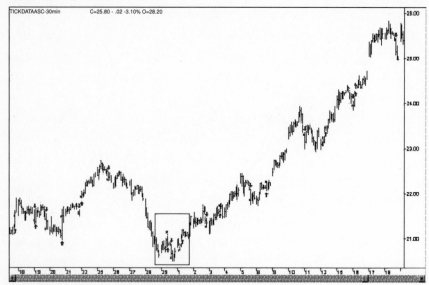

Chart created with TradeStation® 2000i by Omega Research, Inc.

Figure 5.16 Lower risk exposure buying points on November 30–December 1, 1999

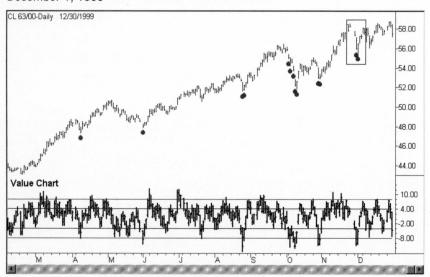

Chart created with TradeStation® 2000i by Omega Research, Inc.

Figure 5.17   Short-term breakout system buy signal on December 1, 1999

Chart created with TradeStation® 2000i by Omega Research, Inc.

to the bull market in crude oil in 1999 is simply to present possible trading system ideas that involve Value Charts and Price Action Profile. It is important to note that any trading strategies presented in this book are not guaranteed to necessarily result in profits. Past performance is not necessarily indicative of future results. Furthermore, there is risk of loss when trading stocks and futures markets.

One important aspect of the trading approach displayed in Figure 5.4, as applied to the crude oil market in 1999, is that most of the winning trades were immediately profitable. From a psychological and emotional standpoint, these types of trading results are ideal because we do not have to endure painful losing periods before becoming profitable. With the development of Value Charts and Price Action Profile, we now have the capability to take these trading rules and scan hundreds of markets (using a computer and trading software) for the purpose of identifying trading opportunities.

UTILIZING VALUE CHARTS AND PRICE ACTION PROFILE IN PYRAMIDING TRADING SYSTEMS

The short-term trading strategy presented in Figure 5.4 can be modified to create a pyramiding trading strategy. We could accomplish this simply by allowing our long-term moving average crossover trading system to be the sell signal for all trades added onto our original position. In other words, instead of exiting our long trades at the +8 Value Chart price level, we could leave them on until our trend-following system generated a sell signal. This would allow us to pyramid onto our original position by simply buying on dips using the trading rules displayed in Figure 5.18. Note that we will still utilize a money management stop, like the trading system in Figure 5.4, for each of our pyramiding trades. The only difference between the trading system in Figure 5.4 and the trading system in Figure 5.18 is that we will not exit the profitable pyramid trades at the +8 Value Chart price level. Instead, we will hold these additional contracts until we receive a sell signal from our moving average trend-following system.

With these new trading rules (see Figure 5.18), we will enter the Crude Oil market when we receive a buy signal from our trend-following moving average system. Previously, in Figure 5.4 the trend-following system was used only as a filter to establish the direction of the trend. There are several rules in pyramiding that we will respect. We will add positions only when the market has trended in a profitable

---

Figure 5.18   Crude oil pyramid trading strategy rules

Buy Signal
Buy highest (high,10) + 1 point stop (applied to a 30-minute crude oil bar chart)

ExitLong Signal
Twenty-five-day simple moving average of the closing prices crosses below a 75-day simple moving average of the closing prices, exitlong all positions. (Applied to daily crude oil bar chart)

Money Management Stop Applied to Pyramid Buy Trades
Place money-management stop 1 tick below lowest low in 30-minute bar chart for the 10 bars preceding the short-term breakout system buy signal.

direction beyond our last entry price level. This insures that we will buy higher bottoms. It is also imperative that we continue to respect the money management stop rules for each individual pyramid trade on the 30-minute bar charts. If we are pyramiding onto our original trend-following entry signal, the market must be moving in the desired direction. It is our goal to keep each of the pyramid entry trades as low risk as possible. An effective way of doing this is utilizing money management stops. The charts displayed in Figures 5.6 through 5.17 will be sufficient for describing how each pyramid entry was executed.

Crude Oil Pyramid Buy Strategy

Initial Buy Signal   Uptrend will be established by a trend-following system. Only follow trading signals in the direction of the trend. When a 25-day simple moving average of the closing prices crosses above a 75-day simple moving average of the closing prices, then buy one contract on the close.

Pyramid Filter (Buy Signal)   Once an uptrend is indicated by the moving average trend-following system (above), look to buy additional crude oil contracts when crude oil trades below the –8 Value Chart price level. As we can see in Figure 5.2, which displays the crude oil Price Action Profile analysis, crude oil trades only below the –8 Value Chart price level 2.83 percent of the time.

Short-Term Trading System for Adding (Pyramiding) Contracts onto Original Position   If the pyramid filter is satisfied, we will use a 10-bar breakout system applied to a 30-minute bar chart to generate our buy signals. This short-term system will be turned on once the crude oil market trades below the –8 Value Chart price level and crude oil is in an uptrend, as defined by the trend-following moving average system. Once the short-term breakout trading system is turned on, we will take the next buy signal. All other subsequent buy signals (generated from the 10-bar breakout system) will be ignored, and all sell signals (generated from the 10-bar breakout system) will be ignored, unless our position has been stopped out.

Table 5.2 Pyramid trading results from the crude oil buy strategy (Figure 5.18)

Reference Charts	Entry Date	Buy Price ($ per barrel)	Exit Date	Exitlong Price ($ per barrel)	Profit/Loss ($)	Risk (Stop) ($)
Figure 5.5	March 8, 1999	12.79	April 15, 1999	26.58	$13,765.00	N/A
Figure 5.6,7	April 9, 1999	15.33	April 16, 1999	26.58	$11,225.00	$635.00
Figure 5.8,9	June 2, 1999	15.61	June 4, 1999	26.58	$10,945.00	$255.00
Figure 5.10,11	August 26, 1999	19.29	September 9, 1999	26.58	$7,265.00	$375.00
Figure 5.12,13	October 6, 1999	22.56	October 7, 1999	21.58	$(1,005.00)	$755.00
Figure 5.12,13	October 11, 1999	20.21	October 25, 1999	26.58	$6,345.00	$635.00
Figure 5.14,15	October 29, 1999	21.14	October 29, 1999	20.58	$(585.00)	$535.00
Figure 5.14,15	November 1, 1999	21.06	November 10, 1999	26.58	$5,495.00	$535.00
Figure 5.16,17	December 1, 1999	24.20	November 11, 1999	26.58	$2,355.00	$555.00

Total Profit/Loss	$55,805.00
Total Profit/Loss from Pyramid Trades	$42,040.00
Average Winning Pyramid Trade	$6,232.86
Average Losing Pyramid Trade	$(795.00)
Average Risk per Pyramid Trade	$535.00
Percent Winning Pyramid Trades	75%

The results from the pyramid trading system displayed in Figure 5.18 are displayed in Table 5.2. As you can see, significant profits can be earned by successfully pyramiding onto a position in a trending market.

Upon reviewing Table 5.2, we observe that the exitlong price for the winning trades is 26.58. The trend-following trading system had not generated a sell signal for this trade. The current market price of crude oil went above the last exit price listed in Table 5.1. For comparison purposes, we will use the last exitlong price listed on the Table 5.1 trading system results table as the market value for crude oil, even though the crude oil market continued trading upward toward higher prices. Both trading systems were subjected to the same commission charges.

As you can see, utilizing the pyramid trading rules displayed in Figure 5.18 has allowed us to build up a seven contract position in the crude oil bull market. In a trending environment, a pyramiding strategy can significantly outperform a short-term strategy that takes profits quickly. It is evident, as we take the results from Table 5.2 and compare them to the results from Table 5.1, that the total profits earned by the pyramid trades ($42,040) are significantly greater than the profits earned by the short-term trading system ($10,090). The average winning trade from the pyramiding trading system was $6,232.86, while the average winning trade from the short-term trading system was $1,946.67.

Again, the purpose of applying the trading strategy displayed in Figure 5.18 to the bull market in crude oil in 1999 is simply to present possible trading system ideas that involve Value Charts and Price Action Profile. It is important to note that any trading strategies presented in this book are not guaranteed to necessarily result in profits. Past performance is not necessarily indicative of future results. Furthermore, there is risk of loss when trading stocks and futures markets. There are numerous ways to utilize Value Charts and Price Action Profile in trading strategies.

6

DESIGNING TRADING SYSTEMS WITH VALUE CHARTS

One of the most powerful applications of Value Charts and Price Action Profile is in the area of trading system development. Every trading system requires *quantifiable values* for the purpose of defining when and at what price level the trading system should enter or exit a market. The most common traditional quantifiable values have been the close of the price bar, the open of the price bar, or a high or low from a previous price bar.

By utilizing Value Charts and Price Action Profile, we now have a whole new set of quantifiable values available to drive trading systems. As you know, Value Charts define relative overbought and relative oversold price levels in any free market with volatility adjusted intervals. These volatility intervals can be used as reference points, or quantifiable values, to direct trading systems when to enter or exit a market.

Figure 6.1 utilizes Value Chart price levels as reference points to identify potentially overbought price levels. A dot appears above each price bar in the top half of Figure 6.1 if the Value Chart price bar penetrates the +8 Value Chart price level in the bottom half of Figure 6.1. It is important to note that only the portion of the Value Chart price bar that exceeds the +8 Value Chart price level is considered significantly overbought. Recall that we utilize the Price Action Profile to

Figure 6.1   Daily Treasury bonds price chart and Value Chart

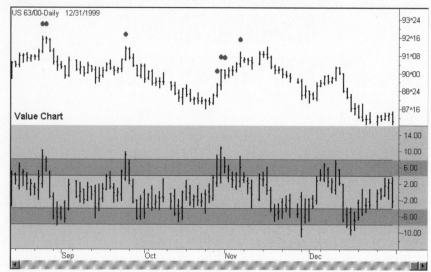

Chart created with TradeStation® 2000i by Omega Research, Inc.

determine how often the Value Chart trades in each Value Chart interval (see Figure 6.2).

Value Charts allowed us to instruct our computer to flag, or identify, any daily price bar that traded above the +8 Value Chart Price level in Figure 6.1. By reviewing Figure 6.2, we know that Treasury bonds only trade above the +8 Value Chart price level 2.29 percent of the time. The ability of Value Charts to provide quantifiable relative price levels to drive trading systems is very powerful and useful to any trading systems developer.

ANALYZING A TREASURY BONDS TREND-FOLLOWING TRADING SYSTEM

One of the most common types of trading systems is the trend-following trading system. Because trends seem to unfold in most markets time and time again, many trading system developers have concentrated their efforts on developing trend-following trading systems. One of the most heavily traded futures markets was the U.S. Treasury bonds market (see Figure 6.3).

Figure 6.2   Price Action Profile from a daily Treasury bonds Value Chart

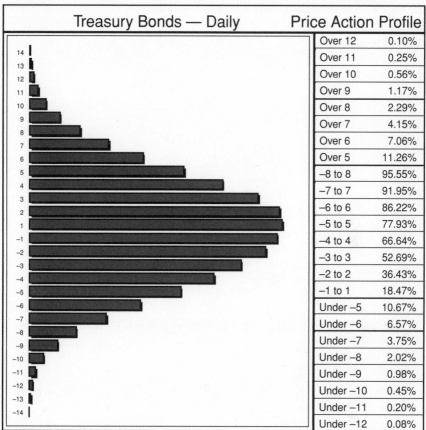

Treasury Bonds — Daily	Price Action Profile	
	Over 12	0.10%
	Over 11	0.25%
	Over 10	0.56%
	Over 9	1.17%
	Over 8	2.29%
	Over 7	4.15%
	Over 6	7.06%
	Over 5	11.26%
	−8 to 8	95.55%
	−7 to 7	91.95%
	−6 to 6	86.22%
	−5 to 5	77.93%
	−4 to 4	66.64%
	−3 to 3	52.69%
	−2 to 2	36.43%
	−1 to 1	18.47%
	Under −5	10.67%
	Under −6	6.57%
	Under −7	3.75%
	Under −8	2.02%
	Under −9	0.98%
	Under −10	0.45%
	Under −11	0.20%
	Under −12	0.08%

As you can see in Figure 6.3, the Treasury bonds market has experienced significant trends over time. We will use this market to illustrate how a basic trend-following system can be improved. Our trading system rules will be very simple. We will utilize a moving average crossover system to generate our buy and sell signals (see trading system rules in Figure 6.4). Moving average trading systems represent one of the most basic trend-following systems. The Treasury bonds market tends to be choppy over time. For this reason, it represents one of the best testing grounds to demonstrate how Value Charts

Figure 6.3   Monthly continuous Treasury bonds price chart

Chart created with TradeStation® 2000i by Omega Research, Inc.

Figure 6.4   Moving average trend-following system rules

Waverage = Weighted Moving Average
Average   = Simple Moving Average

(Buy Signal) If waverage (close, 20) crosses above average (close, 56), then buy one contract at the close.

(Sell Signal) If waverage (close, 20) crosses below average (close, 56), then sell one contract at the close.

and Price Action Profile can be used to improve trend-following systems in choppy market environments.

Note that in Figure 6.4 the basic moving average trend-following system uses the close of the day as the quantifiable value to enter or exit trading positions. This trading system is a stop-and-reverse trading system. In other words, if the trading system is long the Treasury bonds market and generates a sell signal, it will exit the long position and initiate a short position. Most trading systems utilize the open or close of the day to enter or exit trades. One of the weaknesses of trend-following systems is that they tend to buy into markets when they are short-term overbought and sell into markets when they are short-term oversold. This is intuitive from a mathematical standpoint because a market needs to move in a direction by a certain amount in order to establish the beginning of a trend.

The trading rules in Figure 6.4 will be applied to the Treasury bonds market during the time period of August 22, 1977, through December 31, 1999. This represents more than 20 years of trading activity. Furthermore, the trading system will be applied to a continuous forward adjusted daily Treasury bonds daily price chart. Continuous adjusted charts must be created whenever testing a trading system on futures markets because all futures markets have contract months that expire on specified dates, and the different contract months usually trade at different price levels. The chart used for this analysis represents the accurate movement of the Treasury bonds futures market over the specified time period. Several charts will now be displayed that show example trading signals.

The charts displayed in Figure 6.5a, Figure 6.6a, Figure 6.7a, and Figure 6.8a show several trading signals from the moving average trading system displayed in Figure 6.4. The charts displayed in Figure 6.5b, Figure 6.6b, Figure 6.7b, and Figure 6.8b show several trading signals from the *enhanced* moving average trading system described in Figure 6.9. Later in the chapter we review the trading rules for the enhanced moving average trading system and study its corresponding performance results. The charts displaying the moving average trading signals (Figures 6.5a, 6.6a, 6.7a, 6.8a) are placed next to the charts containing the corresponding enhanced moving average trading signals (Figures 6.5b, 6.6b, 6.7b, 6.8b) for the purpose of demonstrating the differences in trade execution price levels. Upon reviewing these charts, notice that the enhanced moving average trading signals often have trades executed at improved price levels, which result in lower risk exposure.

Figure 6.5a Trading signals from moving average system

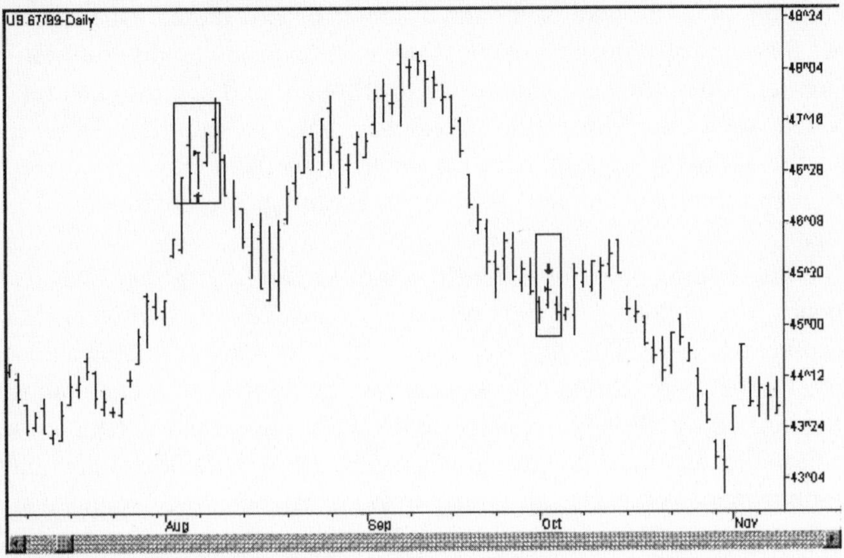

Chart created with TradeStation® 2000i by Omega Research, Inc.

Figure 6.5b Trading signals from *enhanced* moving average system

Chart created with TradeStation® 2000i by Omega Research, Inc.

Figure 6.6a   Trading signals from moving average system

Chart created with TradeStation® 2000i by Omega Research, Inc.

Figure 6.6b   Trading signals from *enhanced* moving average system

Chart created with TradeStation® 2000i by Omega Research, Inc.

Figure 6.7a   Trading signals from moving average system

Chart created with TradeStation® 2000i by Omega Research, Inc.

Figure 6.7b   Trading signals from *enhanced* moving average system

Chart created with TradeStation® 2000i by Omega Research, Inc.

Figure 6.8a   Trading signals from moving average system

Chart created with TradeStation® 2000i by Omega Research, Inc.

Figure 6.8b   Trading signals from *enhanced* moving average system

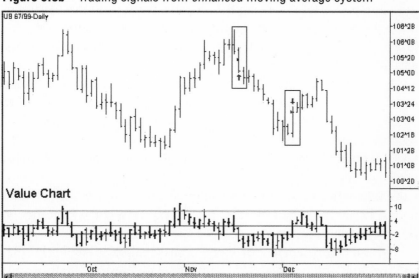

Chart created with TradeStation® 2000i by Omega Research, Inc.

Figure 6.9   Enhanced moving average trend-following system rules

Waverage = weighted moving average
Average   = simple moving average
Value Chart Floating Axis = average ((high + low)/2,5)
Interval = the greater of the two:
          Close − Close[1] (today's close minus yesterday's close) or
          High − Low (today's high minus today's low)
Volatility Intervals = average (interval,5) × (0.2)

(Buy Signal) If waverage (close, 20) crosses above average (close, 56), then buy one contract when the Value Chart price trades at or below the −2 Value Chart price level.

(Sell Signal) If waverage (close, 20) crosses below average (close, 56), then sell one contract when the Value Chart price trades at or above the +2 Value Chart price level.

The charts displayed in Figure 6.5a, Figure 6.6a, Figure 6.7a, and Figure 6.8a show trading signals in the Treasury bonds market generated from the moving average trend-following trading program listed in Figure 6.4. After reviewing the *a* charts, we can see that several of the buy signals appear to be generated at short-term overbought price levels and several of the sell signals appear to be generated at short-term oversold price levels.

Now review the performance characteristics of the trading system in Table 6.1. The moving average trading system generated $63,407.40 in the Treasury bonds market from a time period of roughly 20 years. This trading system traded 105 times for an average profit per trade of $603.88. It was not surprising that the percentage of profitable trades was only 38.1 percent. Trend-following trading systems typically profit only from approximately 40 percent of their trades. In the lower half of Table 6.1 we can review the Price Action Profile Valuation Analysis.

With the development of Value Charts and Price Action Profile, we are now able to evaluate many more interesting performance characteristics of any trading program. For example, the average

Table 6.1   Moving average trading system performance results

Total Net Profit	$ 63,407.40
Gross Profit	$ 208,780.90
Gross Loss	$(145,373.50)
Total Number of Trades	105
Percentage Profitable	38.1%
Number of Winning Trades	40
Number of Losing Trades	65
Largest Winning Trade	$ 20,531.30
Average Winning Trade	$ 5,219.52
Largest Losing Trade	$ (5,218.70)
Average Losing Trade	$ (2,236.52)
Ratio of Average Win/Average Loss	2.33
Average Trade—Win & Loss	$ 603.88

Price Action Profile Valuation Analysis

Average Value Chart Level of Buy Trades	+3.33
Average Value Chart Level of Sell Trades	−2.76

Valuation Determined by Average of Entry and Exit Trades

Number of Trades within Each Category	
Significantly Overbought/Oversold	1
Moderately Overbought/Oversold	36
Fair Value	68
Percentage of Trades Profitable	
Significantly Overbought/Oversold	0.0%
Moderately Overbought/Oversold	33.3%
Fair Value	41.2%
Total Profits from Trades	
Significantly Overbought/Oversold	$ (3,656.00)
Moderately Overbought/Oversold	$ 21,750.70
Fair Value	$ 45,312.70
Average Profit per Trade	
Significantly Overbought/Oversold	$ (3,656.00)
Moderately Overbought/Oversold	$ 604.19
Fair Value	$ 666.36

buy signal, which was always generated on the close of the day, had a Value Chart reading of +3.33. The Treasury bonds Value Chart over the tested period has only traded in and above the +3 Value Chart price level 32.53 percent of the time. This percentage can be easily calculated by adding up all the relative frequency values in and above the +3 Value Chart price interval. The average buy signal, which equated to a +3.33 Value Chart reading, did not appear to be particularly overbought. As we know from the valuation convention established in Figure 3.21, a Value Chart value of +3.33 is considered on the upper end of fair value. It would not be unusual for many trend-following trading systems to register average buy signals in the overbought region of the Value Chart. By reviewing Table 6.1 we can also observe that the average sell signal, which was always generated on the close of the day, had a Value Chart reading of –2.76. Once again, the average sell signal, which equated to a –2.76 Value Chart reading, did not appear to be particularly oversold.

The Price Action Profile Valuation Analysis displayed at the bottom of Table 6.1 was calculated by averaging the absolute value of the entry Value Chart price and the absolute value of the exit Value Chart price. For example, suppose the trading system entered the Treasury bonds at the +6 Value Chart price level and exited several days later at the –4 Value Chart price level. We would simply take the absolute value of both of these Value Chart prices and average them. For this trade we would have an average of +5 ((6 + 4)/2 = 5). Using the convention that we established in Figure 3.21, a +5 Value Chart average reading would fall in the moderately overbought/oversold range.

One interesting fact that the Price Action Profile Valuation Analysis discovered was that 0 percent of the significantly overbought/oversold round turn trades were profitable with a combined net profit of –$3,656.00. Only 33.3 percent of the moderately overbought/oversold round turn trades were profitable with a combined net profit of $21,750.70. Last, 41.2 percent of the fair value round turn trades were profitable with a combined net profit of $45,312.70. The largest winning trade of $20,531.30 happened to be in the moderately over-bought/oversold category. Without this trade the moderately over-bought/oversold group of trades would have had a net profit of $1,219.40, instead of $21,750.70, with an average profit per trade of $33.87, instead of $604.19.

From this analysis we learned that the bulk of our returns came from the round turn trades that fell within the fair value range of the Value Chart. Keep in mind that the analysis from Table 6.1 was derived from one test on one market. The purpose of this analysis is to demonstrate how the Value Charts and Price Action Profile market analysis tools can be used to study and potentially improve trading systems.

ENHANCING A TREASURY BONDS TREND-FOLLOWING TRADING SYSTEM WITH VALUE CHARTS

Now that we have the technology in Value Charts to generate quantifiable values that can be used to drive trading systems, we can enhance the moving average trend-following trading system described in Figure 6.4. We noted that the average buy signal was generated at the +3.33 Value Chart price level and the average sell signal was generated at the −2.76 Value Chart price level. Ideally, we would want to buy into a market at an undervalued (below zero) price level and sell into a market at an overvalued (above zero) price level. Therefore, instead of buying at an average Value Chart price level of +3.33 we could design a trading system to buy at the −2 Value Chart price level. Furthermore, instead of selling at an average Value Chart price level of −2.76 we could design a trading system to sell at the +2 Value Chart price level.

The benefit of buying at slightly undervalued price levels and selling at slightly overvalued price levels is that we should lower our risk exposure to loss and, at the same time, improve the average relative valuation of our trades. Because Value Charts is volatility adjusted and able to generate quantifiable values, we can use it as a valuable trading tool to complement certain trading systems.

The risk of using Value Charts and Price Action Profile to enhance trading systems is in the fact that a market may sharply proceed in the same direction for a time and not bounce back and allow us to enter or exit the market at an improved valuation level. Therefore, in this case, the basic trend-following signal would be better than the enhanced trend-following signal. In long-term investing it is prudent to consider what is statistically likely to happen given normal market conditions. Markets tend to be choppy and sideways more than they tend to trend. Given this fact, Value Charts can operate as a valuable enhancement to many trend-following systems.

There is a degree of error associated with back testing a system that utilizes Value Charts and Price Action Profile. Value Charts is a real-time trading tool. Therefore, as a trading day unfolds, the Value Chart prices corresponding to the current trading day are being calculated from the most current price bar. As the daily trading range expands, the Value Chart volatility intervals will also expand at a much slower rate. Also, as the current trading day expands, the floating axis is also moving in the same direction as price. The floating axis and volatility intervals are calculated from simple moving averages for the purpose of minimizing the impact of the current trading day on Value Chart prices. As the trading day unfolds, the Value Chart prices become more and more accurate. It is believed that this small degree of error in the Value Chart prices of the current trading day can improve fills at one time and can worsen fills at other times. For this experiment we assume that the small degree of error is negligible.

At this time we can review the enhanced moving average trading signals as displayed in Figure 6.5b, Figure 6.6b, Figure 6.7b, and Figure 6.8b. As you can see, the enhanced moving average trading system uses the moving average crossover signal as a filter. If the 20-day weighted moving average crosses above the 56-day simple moving average, the enhanced system will buy the Treasury bonds market once the Value Chart price trades below the –2 Value Chart price level. Therefore, instead of averaging a +3.33 Value Chart price for buy signals, the enhanced system now averages a –2 Value Chart price for buy signals. In the same way, if the 20-day weighted moving average crosses below the 56-day simple moving average, the enhanced system will sell the Treasury bonds market once the Value Chart price trades above the +2 Value Chart price level. Once again, instead of averaging a –2.76 Value Chart price for sell signals, the enhanced system now averages a +2 Value Chart price for sell signals. The enhanced trading system is able to lower the average relative risk exposure for the buy and sell signals and significantly improve the trading results (see Table 6.2).

The most notable improvement in the enhanced moving average trading system over the normal moving average trading system is that it earned a total net profit of $91,461.72 (see Table 6.2) versus $63,407.40 (see Table 6.1). This represents a 44.2 percent improvement in net returns. Commission and slippage for both of these performance tests were not taken into consideration because we are concerned only with the improved performance and not the outright

Table 6.2 Enhanced moving average trading system performance results

Total Net Profit	$ 91,461.72
Gross Profit	$ 208,817.35
Gross Loss	$(117,355.63)
Total Number of Trades	105
Perentage Profitable	41.9%
Number of Winning Trades	44
Number of Losing Trades	61
Largest Winning Trade	$ 21,785.00
Average Winning Trade	$ 4,745.85
Largest Losing Trade	$ (6,166.90)
Average Losing Trade	$ (1,923.86)
Ratio of Average Win/Average Loss	2.47
Average Trade—Win & Loss	$ 871.06
Price Action Profile Valuation Analysis	
Average Value Chart Level of Buy Trades	–2
Average Value Chart Level of Sell Trades	+2
Percentage of Trades Improved	73.3%
Improved Net Profits	44.2%

performances. The profitability from the average trade for the enhanced trading system was $871.06 versus $603.88 for the normal trading system. It is also interesting to note that 73.3 percent (see Table 6.2) of the trades became more profitable with the Value Charts enhanced trading system.

The potential applications of the Value Charts and Price Action Profile concept in the field of trading system development are potentially significant. The analysis of the basic moving average trading system discussed in this chapter is only one example in which the Value Charts and Price Action Profile concept can potentially improve a trading system. The ability of Value Charts to quantify relative price levels opens up a whole world of opportunities in trading system development. The flexibility of Value Charts to adapt to very different markets and also to changing market volatility makes it a very valuable market analysis tool.

USING VALUE CHARTS TO COMBAT WHIPSAWS

One of the weaknesses of every trend-following trading system is its vulnerability to whipsaws in choppy market environments. A *whipsaw* is simply "a situation when a trading system buys into a market at the higher end of the recent trading range and shortly thereafter price falls." In other words, a market moves far enough in a direction to produce a trading signal and once a position is taken, the market retreats putting the position at an instant loss (see Figure 6.10a).

The buy and sell signals in Figure 6.10a, which displays daily price bars from the soybeans futures market, were generated from a stop-and-reverse trend-following system. As you can see, the buy and sell signals in Figure 6.10a were initiated at undesirable relative price levels. An analysis of these trades can be found in Table 6.3.

The trend-following system displayed in Figure 6.10a performed poorly during the choppy soybeans market that unfolded during the summer of 1999. Trend-following systems often incur losses during choppy market conditions. With the development of Value Charts, we have the ability to quantify relative price levels,

Figure 6.10a   Trend-following system whipsawed in soybeans

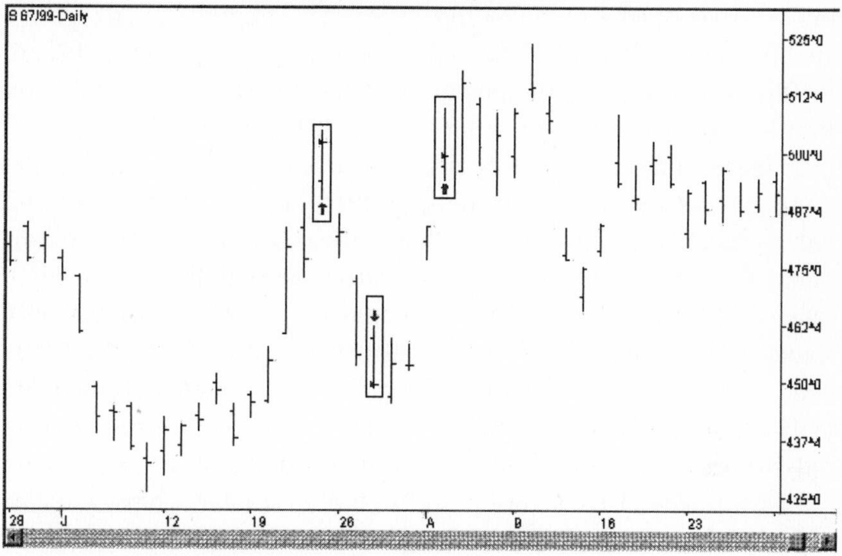

Chart created with TradeStation® 2000i by Omega Research, Inc.

Table 6.3   Value Chart enhancements for whipsaw trades (Figure 6.10a,b)

Trend-Following System (Figure 6.10a)

Date	Trade	Price	Value Chart Price Price Level	Price Action Profile Analysis
23–Jul–99	Buy	502.25	+9.61	1.37% of the time
28–Jul–99	Sell	449.5	−6.51	6.78% of the time
3–Aug–99	Buy	499.25	+9.56	1.37% of the time

Trend-Following System Enhanced by Value Charts (Figure 6.10b)

Date	Trade	Price	Value Chart Price Price Level	Price Improvement Per Contract ($)
28–Jul–99	Buy	451.5	−6	$2,537.50
2–Aug–99	Sell	483.25	+6	$1,687.50
12–Aug–99	Buy	481.75	−6	$ 875.00
Dollars Saved Per Contract from Value Chart Enhancements				$5,100.00

which can potentially improve the performance of our trend-following systems during climates like these. The trading signals generated from the enhanced trend-following system (displayed in Figure 6.10b), which utilizes the power of Value Charts and Price Action Profile, were significantly improved with better entry price levels over the normal trading system. As we can see from Table 6.3, the total savings realized from the improved entry prices was $5,100 per contract. Both of the normal buy signals listed in the top half Table 6.3 were signaled at significantly overbought relative price levels. This is evident by the fact that the soybeans market only traded at or above these overbought relative price levels 1.37 percent of the time. The normal sell signal was generated at a moderately oversold Value Chart price level in which the soybean market only trades at or below 6.78 percent of the time.

Now that we have a very powerful tool to combat whipsaw trades in the markets, we have the challenge of determining when to activate

Figure 6.10b   Value Charts can improve entry and exit prices in choppy markets

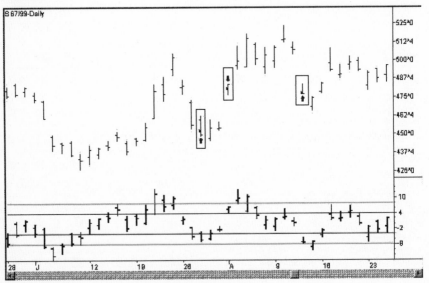

Chart created with TradeStation® 2000i by Omega Research, Inc.

the Value Chart enhanced version of the trend-following trading program. We also have discretion in determining the Value Chart price level at which we will enter a choppy market. Value Charts and Price Action Profile will not always improve the results of a trading system. They do, however, represent powerful tools that can be incorporated into select trading approaches.

7

VALUE CHARTS AND
PATTERN RECOGNITION

In the markets there are often price patterns that form over time and tend to accurately predict the direction of successive price moves. A simple example of a price pattern is the head and shoulders price pattern, where price *is* expected to trade in the direction of the "belt" after the head and shoulders formation has developed (see Figure 7.1).

With the aid of computers, we are able to test any price pattern that we can program in a computer. In order to be legitimate, price patterns, whether simple or complex, must be quantifiable and programmable. A simple example of a quantifiable price pattern is a "price bar reversal up" pattern as shown in Figure 7.2). The price bar reversal up pattern is a two bar price pattern where the second bar has a lower low than the first bar, and the second bar has a higher close than the first bar. If a price bar reversal up pattern is confirmed (as in Figure 7.3), we will buy one contract at the close of the second price bar and then exit our long position at the close of the price bar immediately following this two bar price pattern (the third price bar).

Figure 7.1   Head and shoulders price pattern

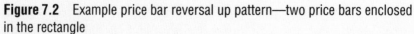

Chart created with TradeStation® 2000i by Omega Research, Inc.

Figure 7.2   Example price bar reversal up pattern—two price bars enclosed in the rectangle

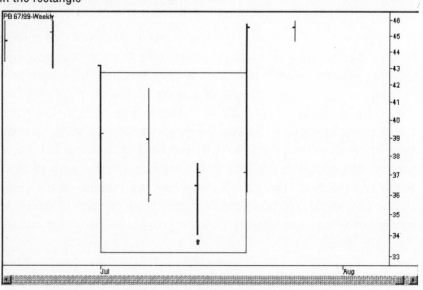

Chart created with TradeStation® 2000i by Omega Research, Inc.

Figure 7.3   Buy signal generated when price bar reversal up pattern is confirmed and exit long signal is generated on the close immediately following the buy signal

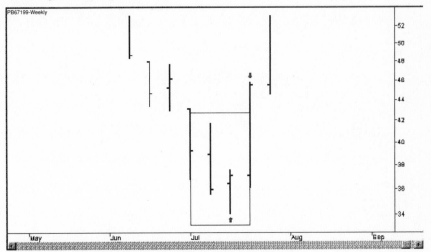

Chart created with TradeStation® 2000i by Omega Research, Inc.

RULES FOR IDENTIFYING THE PRICE BAR REVERSAL PATTERN

Low < Low of 1 bar ago   AND   Close > Close of 1 bar ago

We will use the S&P 500 futures market to test the profitability of the price bar reversal up pattern. A continuous back-adjusted weekly chart will be created for the purpose of testing the profitability of the price bar reversal up pattern as shown in Figure 7.4. It is important to note that we are only able to test patterns that are quantifiable. In other words, testable price patterns are not subjective, but are rather mathematically definable. In our example the price bar reversal up pattern is quantifiable and programmable.

Using the weekly S&P 500 futures chart as just described, we will test the profitability of our pattern between the dates of April 23, 1982, and December 31, 1999.

For the purpose of our tests, we will assume commission to

Figure 7.4   Trading signals generated from the price bar reversal up pattern applied to a continuous back-adjusted weekly S&P 500 futures chart

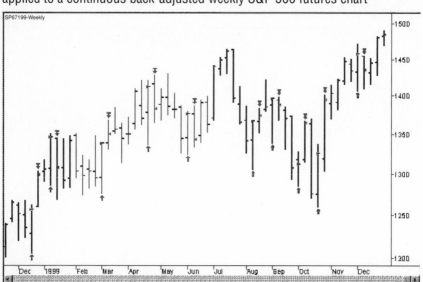

Chart created with TradeStation® 2000i by Omega Research, Inc.

equal $25 per trade and slippage to equal $50 per trade. The price bar reversal up pattern proved to be a very common pattern in the weekly S&P 500 futures chart, which was not very profitable as shown in Figure 7.5. A total of 142 trades were made to earn net profits of $4,512.50. The average trade made $31.78, which is not impressive.

Given the poor results from the test, we can now look to add another filter to our trading signal. Drawing from the power of Value Charts, we can attempt to improve our testing results by adding a Value Chart filter. By doing this, we will become more selective about which price bar reversal up signals to take and hopefully increase our profitability.

The new trading rules will be fairly simple. Utilizing the same rules for the previous test, we will simply add the requirement that the Value Chart low generated from the second day of the price bar

Figure 7.5   Results from testing the price bar reversal up pattern on a continuous back-adjusted weekly S&P 500 futures chart

Strategy Analysis

Net profit	$ 4,512.50	Open position	$ 0.00
Gross profit	$142,562.50	Interest earned	$109,585.08
Gross loss	($138,050.00)	Commission paid	$ 3,550.00
Percent profitable	52.11%	Profit factor	1.03
Ratio avg. win/avg. loss	0.95	Adjusted profit factor	0.81
Annual rate of return	0.26%	Sharpe Ratio	0.07
Return on initial capital	4.51%	Return Retracement Ratio	0.01
Return on max. drawdown	9.65%	K-Ratio	0.15
Buy/hold return	245.24%	RINA Index	(36.57)
Cumulative return	4.34%	Percent in the market	17.12%
Adjusted net profit	($ 28,801.08)	Select net profit	($ 11,812.50)
Adjusted gross profit	$125,989.95	Select gross profit	$112,212.50)
Adjusted gross loss	($154,791,02)	Select gross loss	($124,025.00)

Total Trade Analysis

Number of total trades	142		
Average trade	$31.78	Avg. trade ± 1 STDEV	$ 3,521.88/
			($ 3,458.32)
1 Std. Deviation (STDEV)	$3,490.10	Coefficient of variation	10,982.69%

Run-up

Maximum run-up	$ 18,700.00	Max. run-up date	10/29/99
Average run-up	$ 1,785.56	Avg. trade ± 1 STDEV	$ 4,390.74 /
			$0.00
1 Std. Deviation (STDEV)	$ 2,605.18	Coefficient of variation	145.90%

Drawdown

Maximum drawdown	($ 19,250.00)	Max. drawdown date	1/15/99
Average drawdown	($ 1,887.24)	Avg. trade ± 1 STDEV	$ 0.00 /
			($ 5,146.13)
1 Std. Deviation (STDEV)	$ 3,258.89	Coefficient of variation	172.68%

Reward/Risk Ratios

Net prft/largest loss	0.32	Net prft/max drawdown	0.23
Adj.net prft/largest loss	2.05	Adj.net prft/max drawdown	1.50

Outlier Trades	Total Trades	Profit/Loss
Positive outliers	2	$30,350.00
Negative outliers	1	($14,025.00)
Total outliers	3	$16,325.00

reversal up pattern must penetrate below the –3 Value Chart price level as shown in Figure 7.6. As before, we will exit the trade on the close of the day immediately following the market entry.

By drawing from the power of Value Charts and adding this simple filter, we are able to significantly improve our results as displayed in Figure 7.7. Our new price pattern rules with the Value Charts filter produced net profits of $47,932.50 from 76 trading signals. This equated to a profit of $630.69 per trade, which is significantly larger than the previous $31.78 per trade.

This is one example of how Value Charts can act as an effective filter and improve a pattern recognition trading strategy. The Value Charts filter was able to help us become more selective about which trading signals to take, which ultimately can make us more money.

Figure 7.6 Trading signals generated from the price bar reversal up pattern and the Value Chart filter applied to a continuous adjusted weekly S&P 500 futures chart

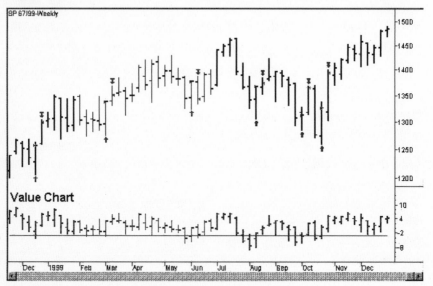

Chart created with TradeStation® 2000i by Omega Research, Inc.

Figure 7.7   Results from testing the price bar reversal up pattern with the Value Chart filter on a continuous adjusted weekly S&P 500 futures chart

Strategy Analysis

Net profit	$ 47,932.50	Open position	$ 0.00
Gross profit	$103,820.00	Interest earned	$132,008.48
Gross loss	($ 55,887.50)	Commission paid	$ 1,900.00
Percent profitable	60.53%	Profit factor	1.86
Ratio avg. win/avg. loss	1.21	Adjusted profit factor	1.34
Annual rate of return	2.36%	Sharpe Ratio	0.31
Return on initial capital	47.93%	Return Retracement Ratio	0.62
Return on max. drawdown	214.58%	K-Ratio	1.62
Buy/hold return	218.68%	RINA Index	237.11
Cumulative return	43.80%	Percent in the market	9.19%
Adjusted net profit	$ 22,421.46	Select net profit	$ 31,607.50
Adjusted gross profit	$ 88,512.58	Select gross profit	$ 73,470.00
Adjusted gross loss	($ 66,091.11)	Select gross loss	($ 41,862.50)

Total Trade Analysis

Number of total trades	76		
Average trade	$ 630.69	Avg. trade ± 1 STDEV	$ 4,498,06/
			($ 3,236.68)
1 Std. Deviation (STDEV)	$ 3,867.37	Coefficient of variation	613.20%

Run-up

Maximum run-up	$ 18,700.00	Max. run-up date	10/29/99
Average run-up	$ 2,212.83	Avg. trade ± 1 STDEV	$ 5,371.77/
			$ 0.00
1 Std. Deviation (STDEV)	$ 3,158.94	Coefficient of variation	142.76%

Drawdown

Maximum drawdown	($ 16,425.00)	Max. drawdown date	8/28/98
Average drawdown	($ 1,450.16)	Avg. trade ± 1 STDEV	$ 0.00/
			($ 4,041.34)
1 Std. Deviation (STDEV)	$ 2,591.17	Coefficient of variation	178.68%

Reward/Risk Ratios

Net prft/largest loss	3.42	Net prft/max drawdown	2.92
Adj. net prft/largest loss	1.60	Adj net prft/max drawdown	1.37

Outlier Trades	Total Trades	Profit/Loss	
Positive outliers	2	$30,350.00	
Negative outliers	1	($14,025.00)	
Total outliers	3	$16,325.00	

Chapter 7 discusses several examples of how Value Charts can be a powerful tool in developing and improving pattern recognition trading strategies. As trading strategies are improved, trading profits should also increase. Although only one basic example was analyzed on how Value Charts can be utilized to improve pattern recognition trading strategies, there are literally thousands more potential applications in this particular area of technical analysis.

8

VALUE SCAN

There are times when we are tracking a group of markets for the purpose of identifying good buying or selling opportunities. A good example of this scenario is when we expect a stock index to appreciate over the next several years and are looking to buy any individual stock contained in the index at an undervalued price. It is difficult to track multiple markets using traditional bar charts and a Value Chart price graphs. Viewing each chart on a single screen can be time consuming. We need a single visual display that can effectively communicate the overbought or oversold state of multiple markets that we are tracking. Value Scan gives us the ability to accomplish this goal.

With the aid of computers and Value Charts, we are able to track thousands of markets, if desired, for the purpose of identifying buying or selling opportunities. Value Scan allows us to visually display the valuation of a group of markets that we are monitoring in a tabular format. This allows us to quickly determine the overbought or oversold state of multiple markets on a single screen. If a market displayed on the Value Scan reaches an undervalued price level that represents a good buying opportunity, we could then display the bar chart and the Value Chart for that market. Value Scan is a powerful tool that condenses information and allows us to efficiently track a large number of markets. Figure 8.1 displays a Citgroup bar chart and Value Chart.

The traditional bar chart and Value Chart in Figure 8.1 represents a common layout for displaying the Value Chart market analysis technique. Although these charts are effective in helping us evaluate Citigroup, they are limited in that they display only price information for one market at a time. Because today's stock markets trade literally thousands of different stocks, we are in need of a tool that can help us sort through a large group of stocks for the purpose of identifying specific buying or selling opportunities. Value Scan was designed to be a powerful sorting tool that allows us to spend most of our time analyzing specific markets that represent immediate opportunities.

Assume that we are looking for buying opportunities in the Dow Jones Industrial Average immediately after the unfortunate terrorist attacks on September 11, 2001. In the wake of these terrorist attacks,

Figure 8.1   Citigroup daily chart above a daily Value Chart where significantly oversold conditions as defined by Value Charts are identified by up arrows

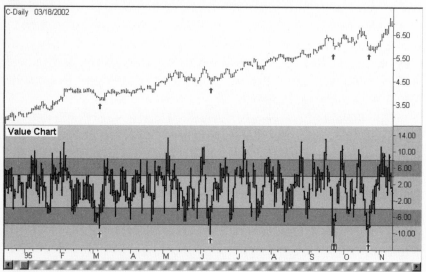

Chart created with TradeStation® 2000i by Omega Research, Inc.

we believe that the Dow Jones Industrial Average has reached an oversold extreme and is likely to experience a rally from current price levels. We are expecting this rally to carry the average higher well into the fourth quarter of 2001. Given this outlook, we are interested in identifying and buying any Dow stocks that are moderately oversold, or moderately undervalued. As described earlier in this book, *moderately oversold price levels* are defined as "any Value Chart trading activity penetrating below the –4 Value Chart price level," which represents a moderately oversold status in which less than 16 percent, theoretically, of the Value Chart trading activity occurs. When this moderately oversold condition exists in one of the Dow stocks that we are tracking, we will buy the stock and hold it for the remainder of the calendar year.

Given the fact that we are interested in simultaneously tracking the overbought or oversold state of the 30 stocks contained in the Dow Jones Industrial Average, we need to utilize the power of Value Scan. The overbought or oversold characteristics of all 30 Dow stocks can be displayed on a single Value Scan table. An example of a Value Scan table is displayed in Figure 8.1. Depending on the exact number of markets that are being tracked on the Value Scan table, it may be necessary to scroll down on the Value Scan table to access information about all the markets.

As you can see when reviewing Table 8.1 the valuation of the closing prices for the 30 Dow Jones stocks is displayed in a tabular format. The Value Scan table displays the stock in the first column, the closing price in the second column, the Value Chart close in the third column, and the market valuation in the fourth column. All of this information is generated from a specific date, which in this example is October 8, 2001. Recall that we are looking for buying opportunities in the Dow stocks. We want to identify stocks that are trading below the –4 Value Chart price level, which represents moderately oversold price activity. As we study the Value Scan table in Table 8.1, we can see that there is only one stock that has closed below the –4 Value Chart price level, and is therefore moderately undervalued (oversold).

It is important to note that a Value Scan table can be structured to

Table 8.1   Value Scan table displaying closing price valuation of the 30 Dow stocks

		Value Chart	Market
ValueScan Sort Instructions: None			*Date: 10/8/2001*
Stock	*Close*	*Close*	*Valuation*
Alcoa Inc. (AA)	$29.91	−3.88	Fair Value
American Express (AXP)	$27.44	−3.71	Fair Value
AT&T Corp. (T)	$19.18	−1.46	Fair Value
Boeing Co. (BA)	$36.45	−2.16	Fair Value
Caterpillar Inc. (CAT)	$46.29	−0.24	Fair Value
Citigroup Inc. (C)	$42.26	−1.23	Fair Value
Coca-Cola (KO)	$46.15	3.02	Fair Value
Disney (DIS)	$18.71	−2.07	Fair Value
Dupont (DD)	$37.35	−0.25	Fair Value
Eastman Kodak Co. (EK)	$33.20	−1.03	Fair Value
Exxon Mobil Corp. (XOM)	$40.71	3.12	Fair Value
General Electric Co. (GE)	$36.80	−2.23	Fair Value
General Motors (GM)	$41.15	−2.09	Fair Value
Hewlett-Packard Co. (HWP)	$16.95	5.09	Moderately Overbought
Home Depot (HD)	$38.37	−2.45	Fair Value
Honeywell International (HON)	$28.34	5.04	Moderately Overbought
Intel Corp. (INTC)	$22.22	4.02	Moderately Overbought
Intl. Business Machines (IBM)	$98.36	4.11	Moderately Overbought
International Paper Co. (IP)	$34.75	0.73	Fair Value
Johnson & Johnson (JNJ)	$55.59	4.34	Moderately Overbought
JP Morgan Chase & Co. (JPM)	$32.44	−6.39	Moderately Oversold
McDonald's Corp. (MCD)	$28.13	0.35	Fair Value
Merck & Co. Inc. (MRK)	$68.60	2.93	Fair Value
Microsoft Corp. (MSFT)	$58.04	4.21	Moderately Overbought
Minnesota Mining & M (MMM)	$97.85	0.05	Fair Value
Philip Morris Inc. (MO)	$50.64	4.72	Moderately Overbought
Procter & Gamble Co. (PG)	$71.87	−0.61	Fair Value
SBC Communication (SBC)	$45.85	0.63	Fair Value
United Technologies (UTX)	$51.67	2.44	Fair Value
Wal-Mart Stores Inc. (WMT)	$51.11	−1.99	Fair Value

display any quantitative information derived from market price activity. In the first Value Scan table, we have chosen to focus on the close of the day from the 30 Dow stocks that we are tracking.

The Value Scan in Table 8.1 displays the Dow stocks in alphabetical order. We can see that most of the stocks closed in the fair value price range on October 8, 2001. We would expect most of the markets on any Value Scan to be trading within the fair value price range, since this range typically contains approximately 68 percent of the Value Chart trading activity. Note that information for each single market is displayed on the rows of the Value Scan table. The column headings are labeled and contain the information that we are interested in monitoring for each market. Note that each user of a Value Scan table can select the group of markets that he or she is interested in tracking (rows) along with the information about each market that he or she is interested in monitoring.

The real power of a Value Scan can be found in its ability to sort the group of markets based on a defined criteria. For example, in Table 8.1 we are interested in identifying markets that are moderately oversold, or trading below the –4 Value Chart price level. As you can see, J.P. Morgan Chase & Company is the only stock that closed in the moderately oversold price range. It would have been much easier to sort these stocks in the order of most oversold to least oversold. By doing this, we could easily have identified the stocks at the top of the Value Scan that met our sort criteria, assuming that several stocks qualified. Take a minute to examine Table 8.2 which contains the Dow Jones stocks sorted from the top down in terms of the most oversold to the most overbought stocks.

The Value Scan in Table 8.2 is much easier to review when it comes to identifying Dow stocks that qualify as moderately oversold. It should be noted that oversold and undervalued are interchangeable, and overbought and overvalued are interchangeable. In a glance, we can see that J.P. Morgan Chase & Company is the only Dow company that is moderately oversold on October 8, 2001. However, the Value Scan in Table 8.3 represents the valuation of the closing prices for the Dow stocks under consideration. Many of the buying opportunities

Table 8.2   Value Scan table displaying a sorted list of the valuation of the closing prices for the 30 Dow stocks

ValueScan Sort Instructions: Undervalued to Overvalued   *Date 10/8/2001*

Stock	Close	Value Chart Close	Market Valuation
JP Morgan Chase & Co. (JPM)	$32.44	−6.39	Moderately Oversold
Alcoa Inc. (AA)	$29.91	−3.88	Fair Value
American Express (AXP)	$27.44	−3.71	Fair Value
Home Depot (HD)	$38.37	−2.45	Fair Value
General Electric Co. (GE)	$36.80	−2.23	Fair Value
General Motors (GM)	$41.15	−2.09	Fair Value
Disney (DIS)	$18.71	−2.07	Fair Value
Wal-Mart Stores Inc. (WMT)	$51.11	−1.99	Fair Value
AT&T Corp. (T)	$19.18	−1.46	Fair Value
Citigroup Inc. (C)	$42.26	−1.23	Fair Value
Eastman Kodak Co. (EK)	$33.20	−1.03	Fair Value
Procter & Gamble Co. (PG)	$71.87	−0.61	Fair Value
Dupont (DD)	$37.35	−0.25	Fair Value
Caterpillar Inc. (CAT)	$46.29	−0.24	Fair Value
Minnesota Mining & M (MMM)	$97.85	0.05	Fair Value
McDonald's Corp. (MCD)	$28.13	0.35	Fair Value
SBC Communication (SBC)	$45.85	0.63	Fair Value
International Paper Co. (IP)	$34.75	0.73	Fair Value
Boeing Co. (BA)	$36.45	2.16	Fair Value
United Technologies (UTX)	$51.67	2.44	Fair Value
Merck & Co. Inc. (MRK)	$68.60	2.93	Fair Value
Coca-Cola (KO)	$46.15	3.02	Fair Value
Exxon Mobil Corp. (XOM)	$40.71	3.12	Fair Value
Intel Corp. (INTC)	$22.22	4.02	Moderately Overbought
Intl. Business Machines (IBM)	$98.36	4.11	Moderately Overbought
Microsoft Corp. (MSFT)	$58.04	4.21	Moderately Overbought
Johnson & Johnson (JNJ)	$55.59	4.34	Moderately Overbought
Philip Morris Inc. (MO)	$50.64	4.72	Moderately Overbought
Honeywell International (HON)	$28.34	5.04	Moderately Overbought
Hewlett-Packard Co. (HWP)	$16.95	5.09	Moderately Overbought

actually take place intraday, or between the opening and closing prices of the day. It would be interesting to know how many of the Dow stocks traded in the moderately oversold price range during the October 8 trading day. We could determine this by creating a Value Scan that tracked and sorted the low prices of the trading days for the Dow stocks listed in Tables 8.1 and 8.2. Table 8.3 displays the low prices, the Value Chart low prices, and the valuations corresponding to the low prices. This Value Scan table is identical to the Value Scan tables in Tables 8.1 and 8.2, except that the low prices are interchanged with the closing prices.

As we review the Value Scan in Table 8.3, it is evident that several Dow stocks traded within the moderately oversold price range during the trading day but closed within the fair value price range. It would therefore stand to reason that if we had bought these stocks when they were trading within the moderately oversold trading range, we would have been profitable by the close of the day. Many trading or investment opportunities occur during the day. Now that we have Value Charts and Value Scan, we have the ability to better capitalize on these intraday buying opportunities because we now have the ability to define *moderately undervalued* and with modern technology and the Internet, an attractive buying opportunity is only an e-mail or a phone page (using a beeper) away.

Now that we can see that many buying or trading opportunities take place during the trading day, how much of an advantage do we have by immediately placing our buy orders during the trading day as soon as a Dow stock dips down and trades within the moderately oversold price range? It would be beneficial to see how we could have benefited by taking advantage of the powerful intraday capabilities of Value Charts and Value Scan. For example, in Table 8.3 we can see that American Express dipped below the fair value price level into the moderately oversold price range for much of the trading session on October 8. However, American Express barely closed within the fair value valuation range. Figure 8.2 charts the trading activity of American Express on October 8.

In the case of American Express, we would not have benefited

Table 8.3 Value Scan table displaying a sorted list of the valuation of the low prices for the 30 Dow stocks

ValueScan Sort Instructions: Undervalued to Overvalued			*Date 10/8/2001*
Stock	*Low*	*Value Chart Low*	*Market Valuation*
JP Morgan Chase & Co. (JPM)	$32.05	−7.99	Moderately Oversold
American Express (AXP)	$26.69	−6.20	Moderately Oversold
AT&T Corp. (T)	$18.69	−5.45	Moderately Oversold
Alcoa Inc. (AA)	$29.67	−4.62	Moderately Oversold
General Electric Co. (GE)	$36.25	−4.33	Moderately Oversold
SBC Communication (SBC)	$44.85	−3.66	Fair Value
Disney (DIS)	$18.41	−3.48	Fair Value
General Motors (GM)	$40.81	−3.41	Fair Value
Home Depot (HD)	$38.15	−3.10	Fair Value
Citigroup Inc. (C)	$41.86	−2.43	Fair Value
Wal-Mart Stores Inc. (WMT)	$50.96	−2.43	Fair Value
Procter & Gamble Co. (PG)	$71.38	−2.18	Fair Value
Eastman Kodak Co. (EK)	$33.00	−1.82	Fair Value
Dupont (DD)	$37.01	−1.76	Fair Value
Minnesota Mining & M (MMM)	$97.10	−1.63	Fair Value
Caterpillar Inc. (CAT)	$45.92	−1.32	Fair Value
Coca-Cola (KO)	$45.36	−0.94	Fair Value
McDonald's Corp. (MCD)	$28.03	−0.44	Fair Value
Exxon Mobil Corp. (XOM)	$39.79	−0.35	Fair Value
Philip Morris Inc. (MO)	$49.72	−0.19	Fair Value
International Paper Co. (IP)	$34.64	0.25	Fair Value
Hewlett-Packard Co. (HWP)	$16.00	0.31	Fair Value
Merck & Co. Inc. (MRK)	$67.78	0.38	Fair Value
Boeing Co. (BA)	$35.77	0.52	Fair Value
United Technologies (UTX)	$50.82	0.53	Fair Value
Honeywell International (HON)	$27.06	0.67	Fair Value
Intel Corp. (INTC)	$21.25	0.84	Fair Value
Intl. Business Machines (IBM)	$96.61	1.08	Fair Value
Johnson & Johnson (JNJ)	$54.87	1.33	Fair Value
Microsoft Corp. (MSFT)	$56.74	1.83	Fair Value

Figure 8.2   American Express traditional bar chart above a Value Chart

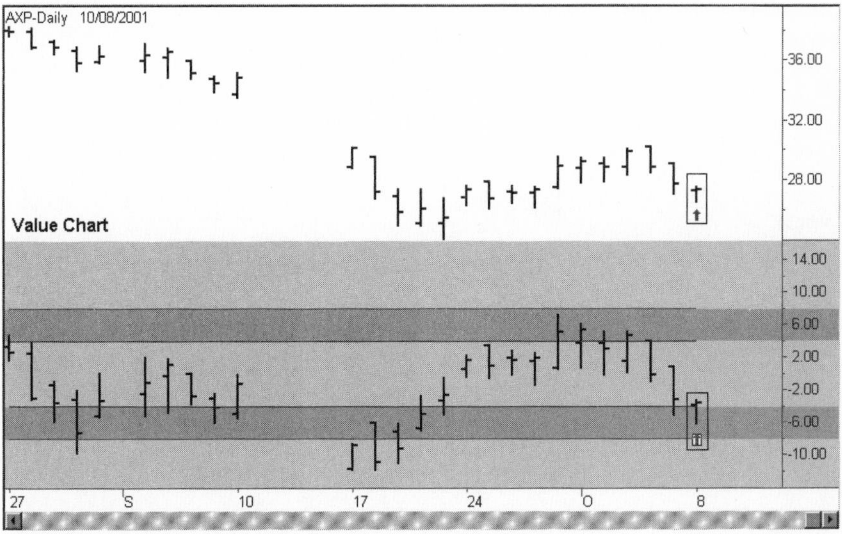

Chart created with TradeStation® 2000i by Omega Research, Inc.

much by buying this stock at the –4 Value Chart price level ($27.27) when compared to buying American Express at the close ($27.36) of the trading session on October 8. However, we can see by reviewing Figure 8.3 that buying American Express anywhere below the –4 Value Chart price level on October 8 would have been a low risk market entry price level. The following trading sessions pushed prices up as high as $31.67 by the fifth trading day.

Notice in Figure 8.3 that the moderately oversold portion of the October 8 American Express price bar represented an ideal point to buy into this stock. It is important to note that Value Charts is a powerful market analysis tool when used in conjunction with other market analysis techniques. Just as certain clubs are effective in certain situations in the game of golf, Value Charts is designed to identify the valuation of a market, whereas other analysis techniques are used to analyze the long-term trend of a market. It will not matter where you buy in a bear market; you are destined to lose money.

Figure 8.3   American Express traditional bar chart above a Value Chart

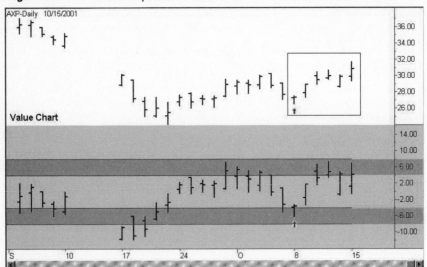

SORTING VALUE SCAN MARKETS

We have learned that we are able to utilize Value Scan to track multiple markets on a single display, or table. When utilizing a Value Scan table, we have the flexibility to dictate how, or in what order, we want the markets displayed. For example, we can rank the Dow stocks listed in Table 8.2 by the degree in which their current price is oversold. In other words, we can display in the first row the market as the most oversold, as defined by Value Charts. The second row will display the market that is the next most oversold stock, and so on. Note that this ability to sort markets according to their degree of being overbought or oversold is a powerful feature. Table 8.2 displays the Dow stocks listed in the Value Scan in Table 8.1 in order of most oversold to least oversold (or most overbought).

We literally have the ability to display the markets being tracked by Value Scan in any desired order. Therefore, we can make sure that the markets that are the closest to generating trading signals are displayed at the top of the Value Scan table and the markets that are not close to generating trading signals are near the bottom of the Value Scan table. We can also display the degree in which each stock is overbought or oversold, as defined by each Price Action Profile. This can be seen in Table 8.4.

Similar to the previous examples, by utilizing the ability to sort the markets listed in the Value Scan displayed in Table 8.4, we are easily able to identify the markets that meet or are close to meeting our trading conditions. If we were looking to buy a stock from a list that we are watching, that is significantly undervalued (oversold), we would be able to see from the Value Scan in Table 8.4 that Allied Signal meets this condition and is fit to buy. Citigroup, DuPont, and American Express are all close to meeting this condition. By sorting the markets so that the stocks closest to trading signals are closest to the top of the Value Scan, we are able to easily track their progress.

Table 8.4 Valuable information about several of the Dow stocks

Symbol	Last	Value Chart	Data Compression	Market Condition	Profile Below	Profile Above
ALD	21.187	−9.74	Daily	Significantly Oversold	1.04%	98.96%
C	16.500	−7.97	Daily	Moderately Oversold	3.90%	96.10%
DD	32.500	−6.66	Daily	Moderately Oversold	6.78%	93.22%
AXP	41.625	−4.04	Daily	Moderately Oversold	16.64%	83.36%
AA	25.187	−0.87	Daily	Fair Value	40.71%	59.29%
CHV	47.750	−0.50	Daily	Fair Value	50.17%	49.83%
BA	33.437	3.80	Daily	Fair Value	76.89%	23.11%
CAT	27.187	4.78	Daily	Moderately Overbought	83.67%	16.33%
DIS	19.250	7.07	Daily	Moderately Overbought	95.69%	4.31%
EK	63.875	8.06	Daily	Significantly Overbought	97.46%	2.54%

UTILIZING INDICATORS WITH VALUE SCAN

A Value Scan table can display Value Chart information along with information generated from any other technical indicators. For example, we could include information generated from a trend-following indicator in our Value Scan table to help identify the long-term direction of the markets listed. If the trend-following indicator is bullish, we would look to buy into the market when the market was moderately oversold or significantly oversold as defined by daily Value Charts. If, on the other hand, the trend-following indicator is bearish, we would look to sell the market when it was moderately overbought or significantly overbought as defined by daily Value Charts.

Our goal in using Value Scan is to have the capability to track multiple markets within one screen. Using any effective indicators or trading systems along with Value Charts and Price Action Profile should further improve our odds and help us realize profits. We are also interested in placing trades that become profitable as close to the inception of the trade as possible. As you know, Value Charts have the ability to identify low risk exposure market entry points in the markets. When we combine the power of Value Charts with other effective trading indicators, we only improve our odds of identifying low risk exposure market entry points. Table 8.5 displays an example of a Value Scan table, which includes a trend-following indicator in addition to information generated from Value Charts.

The Value Scan displayed in Table 8.5 has been designed to track the grain markets along with the pork bellies market. Notice that the daily corn and wheat charts are indicating opportunities to sell into down trends at potentially low risk exposure selling points. By setting up the Value Scan table to track the daily, weekly, and monthly Value Chart price activity, we are able to track the overbought or oversold condition of the listed markets across several different time frames. The daily corn Value Chart is significantly overbought, but the weekly and monthly corn Value Charts are trading at fair value. Notice that the trend of all the grain markets is down. We are therefore looking to trade these markets in the direction of the trend, which is currently down as defined by our trend-

Table 8.5 Value Scan displaying last price, the direction of the long-term trend, the Value Chart price, and the relative valuation for several futures markets

Market	Last	Long-Term Trend	Value Chart	Data Compression	Market Condition	Profile Below	Profile Above
Corn	245.75	Down	8.38	Daily	Significantly Overbought	97.46%	2.54%
Corn	245.75	Down	2.07	Weekly	Fair Value	68.78%	31.22%
Corn	245.75	Down	0.06	Monthly	Fair Value	50.17%	49.83%
Wheat	307.50	Down	8.97	Daily	Significantly Overbought	97.28%	2.72%
Wheat	307.50	Down	0.95	Weekly	Fair Value	51.22%	48.78%
Wheat	307.50	Down	−1.40	Monthly	Fair Value	40.71%	59.29%
Soybeans	495.50	Down	−4.96	Daily	Moderately Overbought	83.67%	16.33%
Soybeans	495.50	Down	−1.32	Weekly	Fair Value	40.71%	59.29%
Soybeans	495.50	Down	−2.34	Monthly	Fair Value	31.68%	68.32%
Pork Bellies	54.53	Up	−0.45	Daily	Fair Value	48.70%	51.30%
Pork Bellies	54.53	Up	−3.29	Weekly	Fair Value	23.57%	76.43%
Pork Bellies	54.53	Up	−1.52	Monthly	Fair Value	39.80%	60.20%

following trading system. Selling short-term overbought price points in a down trend should allow us to enter the markets at low risk exposure points and maximize our potential to profit. Any effective trend-following trading system or indicator can be used in a Value Scan as a filter.

A Value Scan table is designed to condense information, which allows us to track multiple markets on one screen. The Value Charts and Price Action Profile market analysis tools work extremely well with the Value Scan concept because Value Charts are able to define fair value, overbought, and oversold price conditions. This chapter focuses on describing the usefulness of a Value Scan rather than describing the specifics of how to set up a Value Scan table. The universal applications of Value Charts and Price Action Profiles in the field of technical analysis would necessitate that every serious trader obtain Value Charts and Price Action Profile software.

9

USING DYNAMIC VALUATION FOR CHANGING MARKETS

In an early chapter we discuss how Value Charts are created and we demonstrate how Price Action Profiles are used to complement Value Charts. Most of our analysis has centered around developing Price Action Profiles from the entire history of bar chart data for each particular market. However, it is important to investigate other options when we are creating Price Action Profiles and defining the valuation of markets. After all, a strong uptrend will have a unique Price Action Profile when compared to a strong downtrend.

In this chapter we explore the different methodologies that can be used in creating Price Action Profiles and valuation zones. We demonstrate how bull market Price Action Profiles and bull market valuation zones can be applied to markets that are expected to experience powerful uptrends. In addition, we also demonstrate how bear market Price Action Profiles and bear market valuation zones can be applied to markets that are expected to experience powerful downtrends.

CONDITIONAL PRICE ACTION PROFILES

The Price Action Profiles that are discussed in this book thus far have been generated from the entire bar chart history for the market under consideration. Until now, Price Action Profiles have been intentionally generated from as much market data as were reasonably available. The primary reason for this methodology has been to hopefully include data from a complete market cycle. To simply include data from a bull market would not create a Price Action Profile that was representative of the full picture, so to speak. A bull market Price Action Profile can be distinguished from a bear market Price Action Profile in that it would have a positive skew. In contrast, a Price Action Profile generated by using data obtained from a full market cycle should hopefully include enough price history to closely mirror the population. A Price Action Profile created from a sample similar to the population should be the most statistically accurate.

Although Price Action Profiles that are created from a sample similar to the population represent the most accurate long-term profile of Value Chart price behavior, we can often improve the accuracy of Value Charts and Price Action Profiles by tailoring them to specific types of markets. This process involves making a supposition about the type of price behavior we expect to encounter in future trading sessions. In other words, after evaluation of fundamental data or utilizing a trend-following trading system, we might reach the conclusion that a market is likely to develop into a strong upward trend.

In order to observe how we can improve the statistical accuracy of predicting future price behavior by utilizing conditional Price Action Profiles, we take a look at the cocoa futures market. As you can see when viewing Figure 9.1, the cocoa market was in a strong uptrend during the 1970s. The cocoa market then topped out and proceeded to trade in a strong downtrend throughout the 1980s and the 1990s.

The cocoa market displayed in Figure 9.1 has experienced a strong multiyear bull market, a strong multiyear bear market, and numerous periods of choppy, sideways price activity. The daily price data from this market should closely resemble the population of cocoa data. By utilizing the daily price data from the time period represented in Figure 9.1 we could construct a Price Action Profile that should accurately describe the Value Chart price behavior of cocoa. This Price Action Profile can be found in Figure 9.2.

Figure 9.1   Monthly bar chart of the cocoa market

Chart created with TradeStation® 2000i by Omega Research, Inc.

As we analyze the Price Action Profile in Figure 9.2, we can see that this profile closely resembles a normal mound-shaped bell curve. The Price Action Profile appears to be evenly distributed in both the positive and negative Value Chart price intervals. For most applications the Price Action Profile in Figure 9.2, which was derived from a complete market cycle of cocoa, is sufficient. However, when one is able to make a correct supposition about the future trend of a market, he or she has the opportunity to utilize an increasingly accurate conditional Price Action Profile. This is simply a Price Action Profile generated from a defined type of market, which could include an uptrending market, a downtrending market, or a sideways trendless market.

The obvious danger of creating a conditional Price Action Profile is that this type of Price Action Profile increases accuracy only if you are correct about the type of market you are currently experiencing. A conditional Price Action Profile derived from historical uptrends will be increasingly inaccurate if applied to a downtrending market or a sideways market.

Figure 9.2   Price Action Profile from a daily cocoa Value Chart

Cocoa— Daily	Conditional Price Action Profile	
	Over 12	0.15%
	Over 11	0.39%
	Over 10	0.92%
	Over 9	1.84%
	Over 8	3.22%
	Over 7	5.34%
	Over 6	8.24%
	Over 5	12.14%
	−8 to 8	93.71%
	−7 to 7	89.49%
	−6 to 6	83.40%
	−5 to 5	75.04%
	−4 to 4	64.17%
	−3 to 3	50.95%
	−2 to 2	35.51%
	−1 to 1	18.21%
	Under −5	12.61%
	Under −6	8.21%
	Under −7	5.01%
	Under −8	2.91%
	Under −9	1.52%
	Under −10	0.72%
	Under −11	0.30%
	Under −12	0.11%

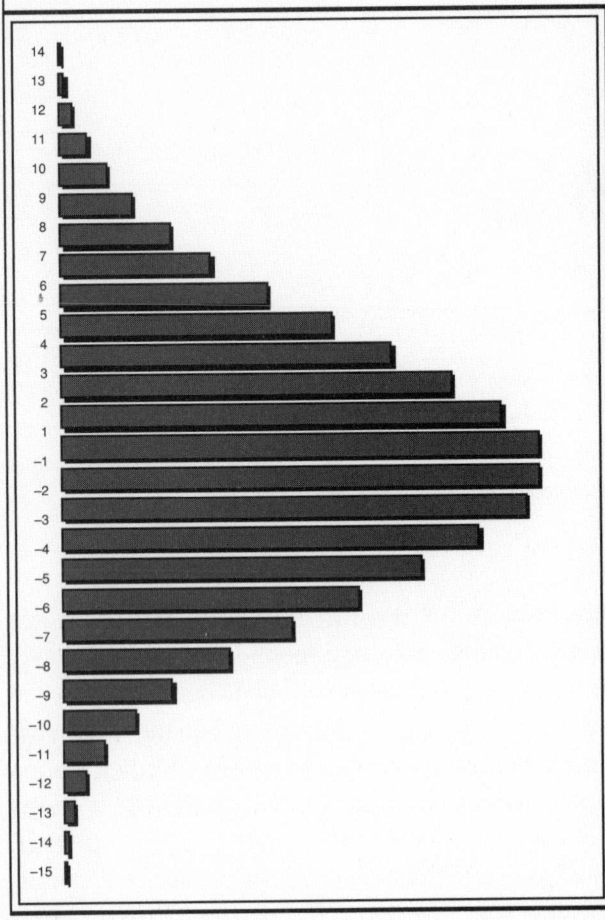

Let's now assume that we are extremely confident that cocoa is about to experience a powerful bull market. Figure 9.3 illustrates the uptrend that unfolded in the cocoa market in the 1975 through 1976 timeframe. The astute investor who forecasted a strong bull market in the cocoa market during this time period could have increased the effectiveness of a cocoa Value Chart by creating a conditional Price Action Profile tailored to a bull market environment.

Figure 9.3 Daily bar chart of the cocoa bull market

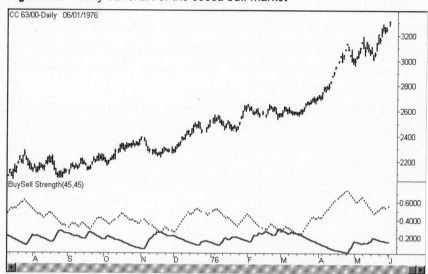

Chart created with TradeStation® 2000i by Omega Research, Inc.

A conditional Price Action Profile customizes the valuation zones on a Value Chart. A conditional Price Action Profile tailored for a bull market environment would be able to better describe the future behavior of the cocoa market assuming that the forecasted bull market unfolded as planned. The reason for increased accuracy is that this conditional Price Action Profile would demonstrate an upward skew and therefore more accurately reflect the upward bias of future cocoa price behavior.

In order to create a conditional Price Action Profile, we need to define the price bar data that need to be collected or utilized. In other words, we need to have the ability to define the bull market environment that we wish to analyze and then only collect price bar data, for the development of our conditional Price Action Profile, when our defined conditions are met. For this example, we will utilize an indicator that measures the buying and selling strength for a market. This indicator, which measures buying and selling strength, is displayed in Figure 9.3. The dotted line represents a 45-day average of the buying strength in the cocoa market and the solid line represents a 45-day average of the selling strength in the cocoa market. We will define a bull market, in this example, as existing when the dotted line (buy strength line) crosses above the solid line (sell strength line). When this bull market condition is met, we will collect price bar data for our conditional Price Action Profile.

A conditional Price Action Profile specifically tailored to a bull market environment would be a more accurate predictor of bull market cocoa price activity, assuming that the projected bull market unfolds as predicted. However, as we stated before, the danger of making a projection or assumption about future price activity is that the assumption could be incorrect. Applying a conditional Price Action Profile tailored for a bull market to a sideways market or a bear market would negate the desired increase in accuracy and ultimately produce significant inaccuracies. As we refine the Value Chart and Price Action Profile market analysis tools for specific types of markets, we incur additional risks if we error in identifying the current market environment. However, the additional potential risks may be acceptable in certain clearly defined situations.

Getting back to the cocoa bull market example, we are able to clearly observe in Figure 9.3 that a significant upward trend unfolded in 1975 and 1976. For this example, we will assume that we correctly projected this bull market in early 1975. Because we are very confident about our bull market prediction in early 1975, we want to generate a conditional Price Action Profile that will reflect our expectations. As we review the cocoa Price Action Profile in Figure 9.2, we note that this profile represents the totality of historical cocoa Value Chart price behavior and forms an even distribution in the positive and negative Value Chart price sectors. This normal Price Action Profile represents cocoa across a complete market cycle. We can now view a conditional Price Action Profile tailored to an uptrending cocoa market in Figure 9.4.

The cocoa Price Action Profile in Figure 9.4 is skewed to the positive Value Chart sectors. Inspection of the analysis to the right of the Price Action Profile in Figure 9.4 indicates that only 8.26 percent of Value Chart price activity traded under the −5 Value Chart

Figure 9.4 Conditional Price Action Profile tailored for a bull market

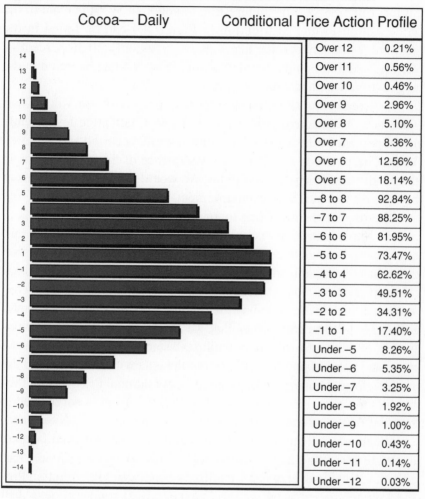

Cocoa— Daily	Conditional Price Action Profile	
	Over 12	0.21%
	Over 11	0.56%
	Over 10	0.46%
	Over 9	2.96%
	Over 8	5.10%
	Over 7	8.36%
	Over 6	12.56%
	Over 5	18.14%
	−8 to 8	92.84%
	−7 to 7	88.25%
	−6 to 6	81.95%
	−5 to 5	73.47%
	−4 to 4	62.62%
	−3 to 3	49.51%
	−2 to 2	34.31%
	−1 to 1	17.40%
	Under −5	8.26%
	Under −6	5.35%
	Under −7	3.25%
	Under −8	1.92%
	Under −9	1.00%
	Under −10	0.43%
	Under −11	0.14%
	Under −12	0.03%

price level while 18.14 percent of Value Chart price activity traded above the +5 Value Chart price level. In contrast, the analysis to the right of the Price Action Profile in Figure 9.2 indicates that 12.53 percent of Value Chart price activity traded under the −5 Value Chart price level, while 12.14 percent of Value Chart price activity traded above the +5 Value Chart price level. The Price Action Profile in Figure 9.4 has a skew toward the positive Value Chart price zones while the Price Action Profile in Figure 9.2 represents an even distribution. Furthermore, it is interesting to note that 59.64 percent of the Price Action Profile distribution in Figure 9.4 can be found in the positive Value Chart price intervals, whereas only 40.36 percent of the Price Action Profile distribution in Figure 9.4 can be found in the negative Value Chart price intervals.

It is interesting to note that only 5.35 percent of the Value Chart price activity occurred below the –6 Value Chart price level, while 12.56 percent of the Value Chart price activity occurred above the +6 Value Chart price level. This is a consequence of the upward skew in the conditional Price Action Profile. We would logically expect this to be the case in a bull market environment.

The final step of utilizing a conditional Price Action Profile is to modify the valuation zones on a cocoa Value Chart to reflect the bull market conditional Price Action Profile. As you recall, the valuation zones have been defined from the statistically accepted standard deviation convention from a normal mound-shaped bell curve. This convention, which is illustrated by the Empirical Rule outlined in Chapter 3 (Figure 3.7) basically states that we would expect to find approximately 68 percent of the data within ±1 standard deviation from the mean and approximately 95 percent of the data within ±2 standard deviations from the mean. When creating a conditional Price Action Profile like the one in Figure 9.4, we find that the mean is not located at zero but rather is found in slightly positive territory.

When we utilize a normal Price Action Profile, we would expect to define fair value as the zone between the –4 and +4 Value Chart price levels. However, when we utilize a conditional Price Action Profile with an upward skew, we would expect the fair value zone to drift into positive territory. Although the Empirical Rule describes the characteristics of a normal mound-shaped bell curve, in the real world, we will discover that Price Action Profiles from different markets will each have a slightly different distribution. Therefore, as we customize the valuation zones (fair value, moderately overbought, etc.) to reflect the bull market distribution of the cocoa conditional Price Action Profile shown in Figure 9.4, we will refer back to the standard distribution (Price Action Profile) found in Figure 9.2 as a point of reference. In other words, the standard cocoa Price Action Profile found in Figure 9.4 defines the portion, or relative frequency, of the Value Chart price activity that we expect to find in the significantly overbought, moderately overbought, fair value, moderately oversold, and significantly oversold valuation zones.

By referencing the cocoa Price Action Profile in Figure 9.2 we are able to establish that 3.22 percent of Value Chart price activity occurred within the significantly overbought Value Chart price region (defined as all Value Chart price activity over the +8 Value Chart price level), 14.17 percent of Value Chart price activity occurred within the moderately overbought Value Chart price region (defined as all Value Chart price activity between the +4 to +8 Value Chart price levels), and 64.17 percent of Value Chart price activity occurred within the fair value Value Chart price region (defined as all Value Chart price activity between the –4 to +4 Value Chart price levels). In addition, we are able to establish that 2.91 percent of Value Chart price activity occurred within the significantly oversold Value Chart price region (defined as all Value Chart price activity below the –8 Value Chart price level), and 15.37 percent of Value Chart price activity occurred within the moderately oversold Value Chart price region (defined as all Value Chart price activity between the –4 to –8 Value Chart price levels).

Using the statistical valuation data from the previous paragraph, we can modify the valuation zones and create a customized Value Chart to reflect unique characteristics of the cocoa bull market conditional Price Action Profile found in Figure 9.4. We know from the previous paragraph that 3.22 percent of normal Price Action Profile distribution (Figure 9.2) occurred within the significantly overbought Value Chart price region, or above the +8 Value Chart price level. We need to determine the specific Value Chart price level that encloses 3.22 percent of the conditional Price Action Profile in Figure 9.4. By inspecting the conditional Price Action Profile in Figure 9.4 and by utilizing extrapolation, we can determine that the +8.88 Value Chart price level and above defines the significantly overbought valuation zone in a bull market customized cocoa Value Chart. We can define the moderately overbought valuation zone in our customized bull market Value Chart as the range between +5.87 to +8.88 Value Chart price levels instead of the range between the +4 to +8 Value Chart price levels in a normal Value Chart. The fair value valuation zone in our customized cocoa bull market Value Chart is defined as the range between –2.85 and +5.87 instead of the range between the –4 to +4 Value Chart price levels in a normal Value Chart. The moderately oversold valuation zone in our customized cocoa bull market Value Chart is defined as the range between –7.24 and –2.85 instead of the range between the –8 to –4 Value Chart price levels in a normal Value Chart. Last, we can define the significantly oversold valuation zone in our customized cocoa bull market Value Chart as the range below –7.24 instead of the range below the –8 Value Chart price level in a normal Value Chart.

Now that we know how to define the new valuation zones for our bull market customized cocoa Value Chart, we can plot this new specialized Value Chart as seen in Figure 9.5. The dotted lines represent

Figure 9.5   Daily bar chart of cocoa above customized bull market Value Chart and trend indicator

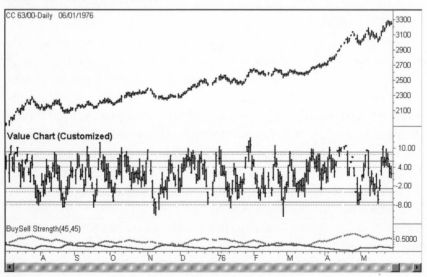

Chart created with TradeStation® 2000i by Omega Research, Inc.

the old Value Chart valuation zones and the solid lines in Figure 9.5 represent the new Value Chart valuation zones as defined by the vocoa conditional Price Action Profile in Figure 9.4. It is important to remember that this new bull market cocoa Value Chart should be utilized only when a bull market is clearly defined by the indicator in Figure 9.3. Recall that we define a bull market as existing when the dotted line, which represents buying strength, is above the solid line, which represents selling strength in the market. Figure 9.5 displays an uptrending daily cocoa bar chart above the customized cocoa Value Chart that reflects the valuation zones from the conditional Price Action Profile in Figure 9.4. Figure 9.4 also displays the trend-following indicator from Figure 9.3 on the bottom of the chart. Figure 9.6 displays the identical bar chart and Value Chart found in Figure 9.5 but does not contain the trend-following indicator at the bottom. By removing the trend-following indicator in Figure 9.6 we are better able to view the customized bull market Value Chart.

Figure 9.6 Daily bar chart of cocoa above customized bull market Value Chart

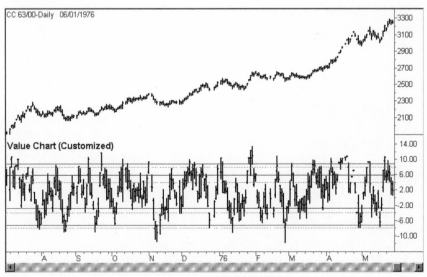

Chart created with TradeStation® 2000i by Omega Research, Inc.

The customized Value Chart displayed in Figures 9.5 and 9.6 will offer a more statistically accurate distribution when applied to an uptrending market as opposed to the normal Value Chart with normal valuation zones. The ability to generate a more accurate valuation of a market allows us to be more precise when identifying trading opportunities and investment opportunities. For example, we can take this customized valuation of the uptrending cocoa market and place a dot below any price bars that trade below the −7.24 Value Chart price level, which signifies trading activity within the significantly oversold Value Chart valuation zone as illustrated in Figure 9.7. This allows us to potentially identify excellent market entry points with very low risk exposure. By entering the cocoa bull market at low risk exposure points, we gain the advantage of often having our trade or investment become profitable almost immediately after the inception of the trade.

Figure 9.7   Daily bar chart of cocoa above customized bull market Value Chart where dots identify price bars that trade within the significantly oversold Value Chart price zone

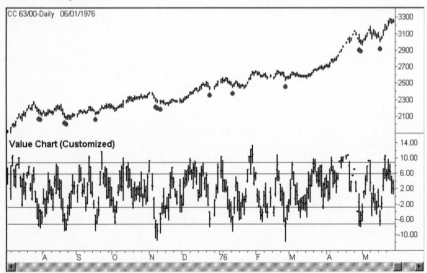

Chart created with TradeStation® 2000i by Omega Research, Inc.

Conditional Price Action Profiles and customized Value Chart price zones have many potential applications in stock, bonds, currencies, and futures markets. We could have spent a significant portion of this book addressing this topic. The cocoa bull market example has demonstrated how we can further increase the accuracy of Value Charts when applied to defined market conditions, such as a bull market environment. With the aid of computer technology we will literally be able explore thousands of different conditional Price Action Profile applications, if desired.

10

DOLLAR COST AVERAGING WITH VALUE CHARTS

Many investment professionals have used dollar cost averaging as a strategy to minimize systemic risk and market risk when entering into a position. Dollar cost averaging is usually associated with long-term investing in the stock market. This technique is usually embraced by investors who are not market timers. Unlike market timers, these investors believe that it is nearly impossible to identify the highs and lows in a market over time. With the advent of Value Charts, we are now able to identify the valuation of a market. We are now able to clearly identify moderately undervalued (oversold) and significantly undervalued (oversold) price levels with the assistance of Value Charts and Price Action Profiles. This chapter explores how Value Charts can also be used, along with dollar cost averaging, to minimize market and systemic risk when we are accumulating stock. Although we explore different examples using stocks in the chapter, these strategies can be applied to any liquid standardized market in the world.

DOLLAR COST AVERAGING

The object of dollar cost averaging is to invest a defined amount of money at regular intervals in the market so the average cost of shares tends to even out the market's peaks and troughs. As you enter the market over time with this strategy, a defined invested dollar amount will purchase fewer shares when the market is up and more shares when the market is down. While an investor will not achieve the positive results of buying at the market's low point and selling at its high point, neither will he suffer the consequences of buying at the market's high point and selling at the low point. The primary goal of this strategy is, on average, to accumulate a position in a market while paying a fair price for the accumulated shares of stock. Some investors also prefer the dollar cost averaging strategy because it removes the emotions from having to make correct decisions about when to enter or exit a market. This strategy is systematic in nature and relatively easy to follow.

For our example, we want to buy $100,000 dollars of Alcoa stock over the upcoming months. A bar chart of Alcoa is displayed in Figure 10.1. Although we are bullish longer term on this stock, we want to be cautious and accumulate our position using dollar cost averaging. We

Figure 10.1   Daily bar chart of Alcoa stock

Chart created with TradeStation® 2000i by Omega Research, Inc.

will begin accumulating this stock January 1, 2001, and continue our acquisition in five phases. Using the dollar cost averaging approach, we will buy $20,000 of Alcoa stock at the close of trading on January 1 and continue buying $20,000 blocks at the close of trading on the first of the following four months (February 1, March 1, April 1, and May 1). If the first of a month lies on a weekend, we will purchase the $20,000 block of stock at the close of the first trading session of that month. On May 1, we will have completed our acquisition of Alcoa stock. As stated before, the dollar cost averaging approach is not concerned about timing any market entries, but rather seeks to achieve a fair average purchase price over time.

Now that we have Value Charts and Price Action Profiles, we will also examine an alternative strategy that utilizes these powerful market analysis tools to enter Alcoa stock. Similar to the dollar cost averaging example, we will purchase $100,000 of Alcoa stock in five $20,000 blocks. Unlike the dollar cost averaging strategy, however, we will concern ourselves with market timing. Now that we have the ability to define and identify significantly oversold price levels real time, we will enter into our five positions at the first five opportunities when Alcoa stock trades within the significantly oversold valuation zone. Because our goal for both of these strategies is the same, that being to avoid the market and systemic risk associated with entering a market in one lump sum, we will not enter two $20,000 blocks during one trough. In other words, if Alcoa trades within the significantly oversold valuation zone on two consecutive days or on several days during the same trough, we invest only during the first session that trades within the significantly oversold valuation zone.

The chart in Figure 10.2 identifies each of the five days when the dollar cost average strategy entered into Alcoa stock. These entry points in Figure 10.2 are identified with dots underneath the appropriate price bars. The Value Chart stock accumulation strategy is displayed in Figure 10.3 and Figure 10.4, where dots flag the entry price bars. Unlike the dollar cost averaging strategy, which enters each of the five positions at the close of each trading session, the Value Chart accumulation strategy enters each position at the price level in each entry bar that corresponds with the –8 Value Chart price level. The

Figure 10.2   Daily bar chart of Alcoa stock with flagged dollar cost average entry points

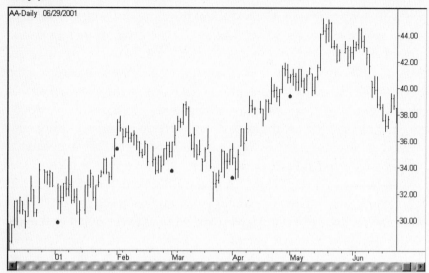

Chart created with TradeStation® 2000i by Omega Research, Inc.

Figure 10.3   Daily bar chart of Alcoa stock with flagged Value Chart entry points

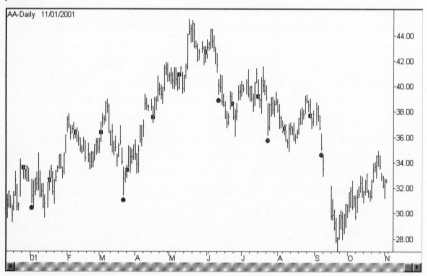

Chart created with TradeStation® 2000i by Omega Research, Inc.

Figure 10.4 Daily bar chart and Value Chart of Alcoa stock with flagged Value Chart entry points

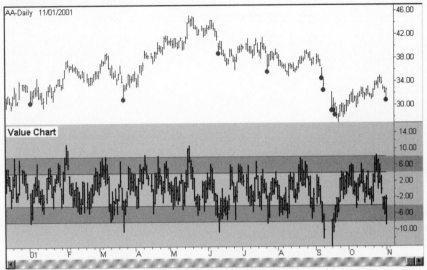

Chart created with TradeStation® 2000i by Omega Research, Inc.

dollar cost averaging strategy was fully invested by May 1, 2001, whereas the Value Chart accumulation strategy was fully invested by September 7, 2001. Figure 10.4 is identical to Figure 10.3 except it displays the Value Chart below the Alcoa price chart.

Recall that each entry point in both the dollar cost averaging strategy and the Value Chart accumulation strategy represents a purchase of $20,000 of stock. If the entry price was cheaper, more shares of Alcoa were purchased. If the purchase price was more expensive, fewer shares of Alcoa were purchased. When comparing the two strategies, it makes sense that the Value Chart accumulation strategy would typically take longer to implement because Alcoa trades only below the −8 Value Chart price level 2.93 percent of the time. The Alcoa Price Action Profile can be found in Figure 10.5. It is not surprising that it took Alcoa nine months to penetrate the significantly oversold price level five times. As you can see when inspecting Figure 10.3 and Figure 10.4, the five Value Chart accumulation points were fairly evenly

Figure 10.5   Price Action Profile from a daily Alcoa Value Chart

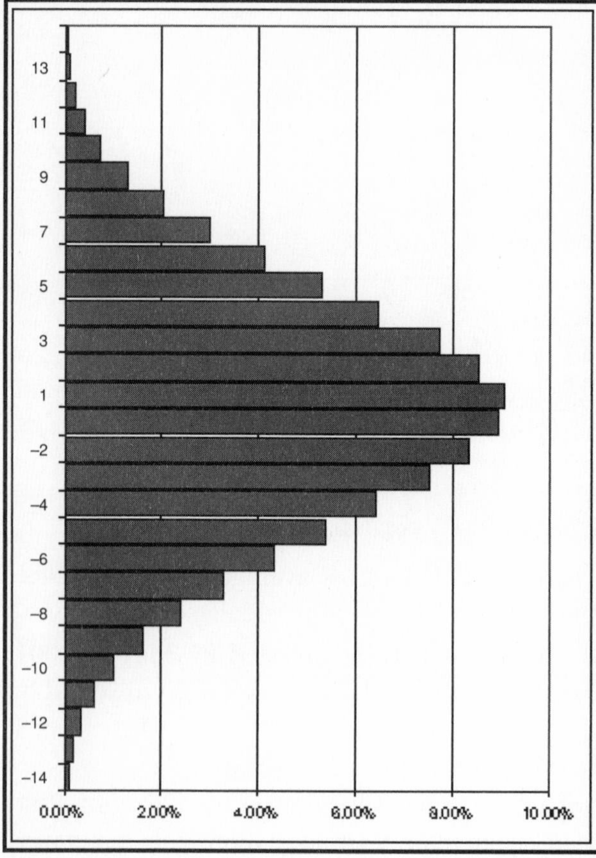

Alcoa (AA)— Daily	Price Action Profile	
	Over 12	0.30%
	Over 11	0.65%
	Over 10	1.28%
	Over 9	2.32%
	Over 8	3.97%
	Over 7	6.38%
	Over 6	9.71%
	Over 5	14.04%
	−8 to 8	99.48%
	−7 to 7	93.07%
	−6 to 6	82.21%
	−5 to 5	73.76%
	−4 to 4	63.01%
	−3 to 3	50.12%
	−2 to 2	34.88%
	−1 to 1	18.00%
	Under −5	12.17%
	Under −6	8.04%
	Under −7	4.99%
	Under −8	2.93%
	Under −9	1.61%
	Under −10	0.85%
	Under −11	0.41%
	Under −12	0.18%

spread out. This is a coincidence and does not necessarily represent a model for what we expect to be normal.

Before we go on, it is important to recognize the risk and reward associated with each of the investment entry strategies that we are analyzing. A risk associated with the dollar cost averaging strategy is that market entries may occur during market peaks and may represent moderately overbought or significantly overbought price levels. This strategy is not concerned with timing market entries but is predicated upon the idea that the average price paid for the accumulated stock will be reasonable and fair. The statistical likelihood of entering the stock over time at all the peaks or all the troughs is very slim. This strategy is generally effective at achieving, on average, a fair average cost and is generally effective in avoiding market risk and systemic risk associated with entering a position at a single price level. A risk associated with entering a stock position using the Value Chart accumulation technique is that the market may not trade below the Value Chart price level entry point frequently enough to allow an investor to enter part or all of a position.

The two strategies can now be compared in Table 10a and Table 10b. The five $20,000 stock purchases made by the dollar cost average accumulation strategy paid an average price of $36.21 per share. The five $20,000 stock purchases made by the Value Charts accumulation strategy paid an average price of $34.99 per share. The Value Charts strategy paid approximately $1.22 less per share than the dollar cost average strategy. Furthermore, the Value Charts strategy accumulated 2,881 shares whereas the dollar cost average strategy accumulated 2,782 shares. The ending account value calculated on November 30, 2001, with a closing price in Alcoa stock of $38.60 was $107,339.25, less commission for the dollar cost average strategy and

Table 10.1a Comparing results from purchases made by dollar cost average strategy versus Value Charts strategy

Dollar Cost Averaging Accumulation Strategy			
Date	Price per Share	Purchase Amount	Shares
1/2/01	$31.56	$20,000	633.71
2/1/01	$37.55	$20,000	532.62
3/1/01	$36.03	$20,000	555.09
4/1/01	$34.86	$20,000	573.72
5/1/01	$41.05	$20,000	487.21
		Total Shares	2,782.36
		Price per share on 11/30/00	$38.60
		Total value of stock on 11/30/01	$107,399.25

Table 10.1b   Comparing results from purchases made by dollar cost average strategy versus Value Charts strategy

Value Chart Accumulation Strategy

Date	Price per Share	Purchase Amount	Shares
1/02/01	$31.00	$20,000	645.16
3/22/01	$32.24	$20,000	620.35
6/12/01	$40.14	$20,000	498.26
7/24/01	$36.42	$20,000	549.15
9/07/01	$35.16	$20,000	568.83
		Total Shares	2,881.74
	Price per share on 11/30/00		$38.60
	Total value of stock on 11/30/01		$111,235.23

$111,227.81, less commission for the Value Charts strategy. This equates to an increase in profits of $3,828.56 when having used the Value Charts strategy versus the dollar cost averaging strategy. These profits represent a 3.82 percent greater return when having used the Value Charts strategy versus the dollar cost averaging strategy. Depending on the size of the investment, the improved returns can equate to a significant increase in profits when considering one strategy over the other.

When using Value Charts as a tool to scale into a market, there are literally hundreds of different variations of strategies that one can follow. It is evident that the Value Charts accumulation strategy is a viable strategy when we are scaling into the market. The patience required to wait until a clearly defined buying opportunity as defined by Value Charts can pay big dividends, especially when working with sizable accounts. With the advent of Value Charts and Price Action Profile, we now have powerful tools that can help us strategically time our entries into any market.

Appendix
PRICE ACTION PROFILES OF DOW 30 STOCKS

Ihe following include Price Action Profiles for each of the Dow 30 stocks (Figures A.1–A.30). Each Price Action Profile was generated from as much daily bar chart data as were reasonably accessible. It is important to note that two Price Action Profiles generated from the same stock (or market) can vary depending on the volume of price data (length of each time period) that were used to generate each profile.

Figure A.1 ALCOA INC (AA)—Daily Price Action Profile

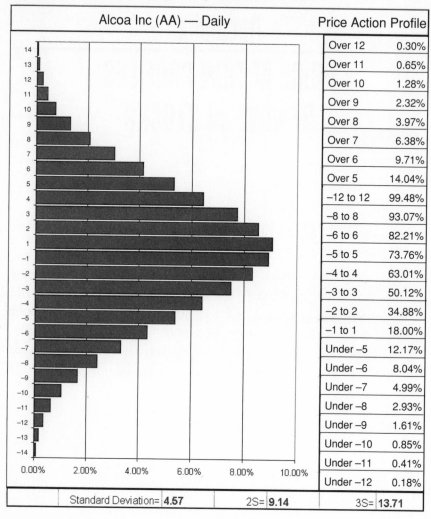

Alcoa Inc (AA) — Daily	Price Action Profile	
	Over 12	0.30%
	Over 11	0.65%
	Over 10	1.28%
	Over 9	2.32%
	Over 8	3.97%
	Over 7	6.38%
	Over 6	9.71%
	Over 5	14.04%
	−12 to 12	99.48%
	−8 to 8	93.07%
	−6 to 6	82.21%
	−5 to 5	73.76%
	−4 to 4	63.01%
	−3 to 3	50.12%
	−2 to 2	34.88%
	−1 to 1	18.00%
	Under −5	12.17%
	Under −6	8.04%
	Under −7	4.99%
	Under −8	2.93%
	Under −9	1.61%
	Under −10	0.85%
	Under −11	0.41%
	Under −12	0.18%
Standard Deviation= **4.57**	2S= **9.14**	3S= **13.71**

Figure A.2 AMERICAN EXPRESS CO (AXP)—Daily Price Action Profile

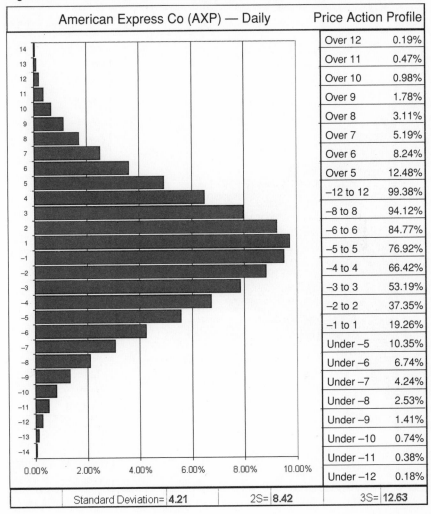

American Express Co (AXP) — Daily	Price Action Profile	
	Over 12	0.19%
	Over 11	0.47%
	Over 10	0.98%
	Over 9	1.78%
	Over 8	3.11%
	Over 7	5.19%
	Over 6	8.24%
	Over 5	12.48%
	−12 to 12	99.38%
	−8 to 8	94.12%
	−6 to 6	84.77%
	−5 to 5	76.92%
	−4 to 4	66.42%
	−3 to 3	53.19%
	−2 to 2	37.35%
	−1 to 1	19.26%
	Under −5	10.35%
	Under −6	6.74%
	Under −7	4.24%
	Under −8	2.53%
	Under −9	1.41%
	Under −10	0.74%
	Under −11	0.38%
	Under −12	0.18%
Standard Deviation= **4.21**	2S= **8.42**	3S= **12.63**

Figure A.3   AT&T CORP (T)—Daily Price Action Profile

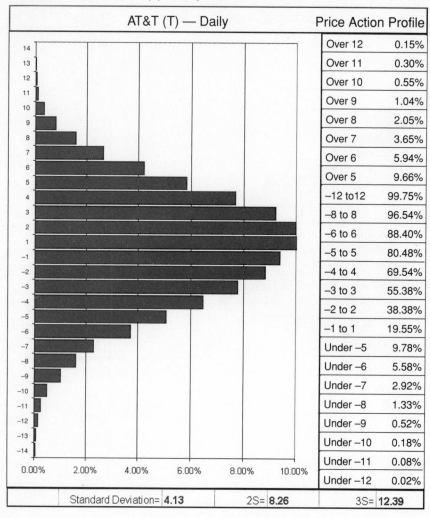

AT&T (T) — Daily	Price Action Profile	
	Over 12	0.15%
	Over 11	0.30%
	Over 10	0.55%
	Over 9	1.04%
	Over 8	2.05%
	Over 7	3.65%
	Over 6	5.94%
	Over 5	9.66%
	−12 to12	99.75%
	−8 to 8	96.54%
	−6 to 6	88.40%
	−5 to 5	80.48%
	−4 to 4	69.54%
	−3 to 3	55.38%
	−2 to 2	38.38%
	−1 to 1	19.55%
	Under −5	9.78%
	Under −6	5.58%
	Under −7	2.92%
	Under −8	1.33%
	Under −9	0.52%
	Under −10	0.18%
	Under −11	0.08%
	Under −12	0.02%
Standard Deviation= **4.13**	2S= **8.26**	3S= **12.39**

Figure A.4   BOEING CO (BA)—Daily Price Action Profile

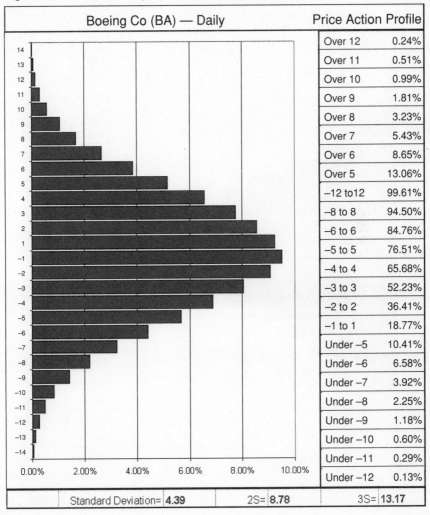

Boeing Co (BA) — Daily	Price Action Profile	
	Over 12	0.24%
	Over 11	0.51%
	Over 10	0.99%
	Over 9	1.81%
	Over 8	3.23%
	Over 7	5.43%
	Over 6	8.65%
	Over 5	13.06%
	−12 to12	99.61%
	−8 to 8	94.50%
	−6 to 6	84.76%
	−5 to 5	76.51%
	−4 to 4	65.68%
	−3 to 3	52.23%
	−2 to 2	36.41%
	−1 to 1	18.77%
	Under −5	10.41%
	Under −6	6.58%
	Under −7	3.92%
	Under −8	2.25%
	Under −9	1.18%
	Under −10	0.60%
	Under −11	0.29%
	Under −12	0.13%

| Standard Deviation= **4.39** | 2S= **8.78** | 3S= **13.17** |

Figure A.5 CATERPILLAR INC (CAT)—Daily Price Action Profile

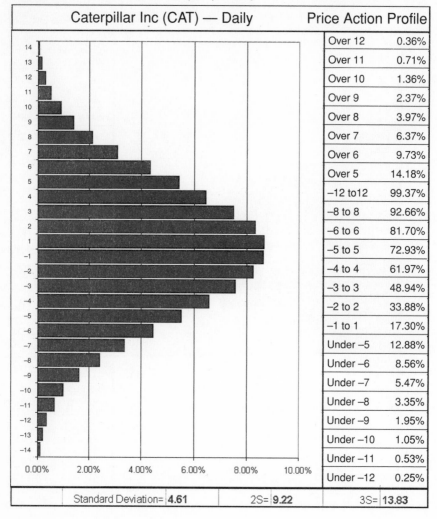

Caterpillar Inc (CAT) — Daily	Price Action Profile	
	Over 12	0.36%
	Over 11	0.71%
	Over 10	1.36%
	Over 9	2.37%
	Over 8	3.97%
	Over 7	6.37%
	Over 6	9.73%
	Over 5	14.18%
	−12 to12	99.37%
	−8 to 8	92.66%
	−6 to 6	81.70%
	−5 to 5	72.93%
	−4 to 4	61.97%
	−3 to 3	48.94%
	−2 to 2	33.88%
	−1 to 1	17.30%
	Under −5	12.88%
	Under −6	8.56%
	Under −7	5.47%
	Under −8	3.35%
	Under −9	1.95%
	Under −10	1.05%
	Under −11	0.53%
	Under −12	0.25%

| Standard Deviation= **4.61** | 2S= **9.22** | 3S= **13.83** |

Figure A.6 CITIGROUP INC (C)—Daily Price Action Profile

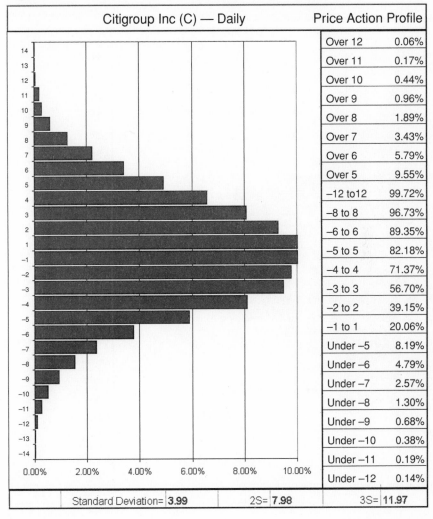

Citigroup Inc (C) — Daily	Price Action Profile	
	Over 12	0.06%
	Over 11	0.17%
	Over 10	0.44%
	Over 9	0.96%
	Over 8	1.89%
	Over 7	3.43%
	Over 6	5.79%
	Over 5	9.55%
	−12 to12	99.72%
	−8 to 8	96.73%
	−6 to 6	89.35%
	−5 to 5	82.18%
	−4 to 4	71.37%
	−3 to 3	56.70%
	−2 to 2	39.15%
	−1 to 1	20.06%
	Under −5	8.19%
	Under −6	4.79%
	Under −7	2.57%
	Under −8	1.30%
	Under −9	0.68%
	Under −10	0.38%
	Under −11	0.19%
	Under −12	0.14%

Standard Deviation= **3.99**   2S= **7.98**   3S= **11.97**

Figure A.7 COCA-COLA CO (KO)—Daily Price Action Profile

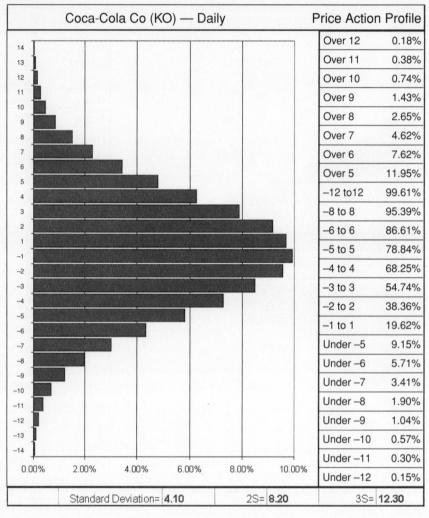

Coca-Cola Co (KO) — Daily	Price Action Profile	
	Over 12	0.18%
	Over 11	0.38%
	Over 10	0.74%
	Over 9	1.43%
	Over 8	2.65%
	Over 7	4.62%
	Over 6	7.62%
	Over 5	11.95%
	−12 to 12	99.61%
	−8 to 8	95.39%
	−6 to 6	86.61%
	−5 to 5	78.84%
	−4 to 4	68.25%
	−3 to 3	54.74%
	−2 to 2	38.36%
	−1 to 1	19.62%
	Under −5	9.15%
	Under −6	5.71%
	Under −7	3.41%
	Under −8	1.90%
	Under −9	1.04%
	Under −10	0.57%
	Under −11	0.30%
	Under −12	0.15%

| Standard Deviation= **4.10** | 2S= **8.20** | 3S= **12.30** |

Figure A.8   WALT DISNEY HLDG CO (DIS)—Daily Price Action Profile

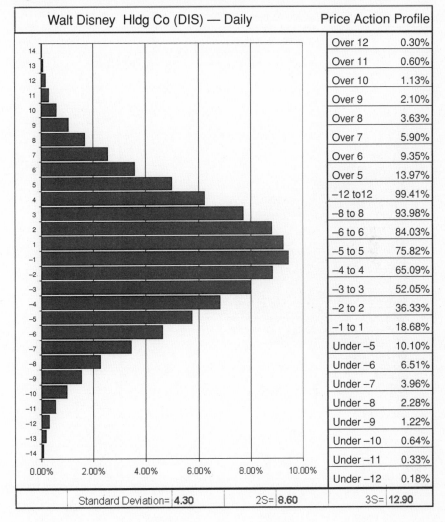

Walt Disney Hldg Co (DIS) — Daily	Price Action Profile	
	Over 12	0.30%
	Over 11	0.60%
	Over 10	1.13%
	Over 9	2.10%
	Over 8	3.63%
	Over 7	5.90%
	Over 6	9.35%
	Over 5	13.97%
	−12 to12	99.41%
	−8 to 8	93.98%
	−6 to 6	84.03%
	−5 to 5	75.82%
	−4 to 4	65.09%
	−3 to 3	52.05%
	−2 to 2	36.33%
	−1 to 1	18.68%
	Under −5	10.10%
	Under −6	6.51%
	Under −7	3.96%
	Under −8	2.28%
	Under −9	1.22%
	Under −10	0.64%
	Under −11	0.33%
	Under −12	0.18%
Standard Deviation= **4.30**	2S= **8.60**	3S= **12.90**

Figure A.9 E.I. DU PONT DE NEMOURS CO (DD)—Daily Price Action Profile

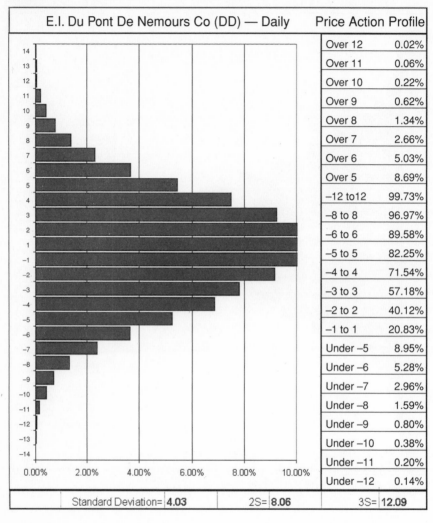

E.I. Du Pont De Nemours Co (DD) — Daily	Price Action Profile	
	Over 12	0.02%
	Over 11	0.06%
	Over 10	0.22%
	Over 9	0.62%
	Over 8	1.34%
	Over 7	2.66%
	Over 6	5.03%
	Over 5	8.69%
	−12 to12	99.73%
	−8 to 8	96.97%
	−6 to 6	89.58%
	−5 to 5	82.25%
	−4 to 4	71.54%
	−3 to 3	57.18%
	−2 to 2	40.12%
	−1 to 1	20.83%
	Under −5	8.95%
	Under −6	5.28%
	Under −7	2.96%
	Under −8	1.59%
	Under −9	0.80%
	Under −10	0.38%
	Under −11	0.20%
	Under −12	0.14%
Standard Deviation= **4.03**	2S= **8.06**	3S= **12.09**

Figure A.10 EASTMAN KODAK CO (EK)—Daily Price Action Profile

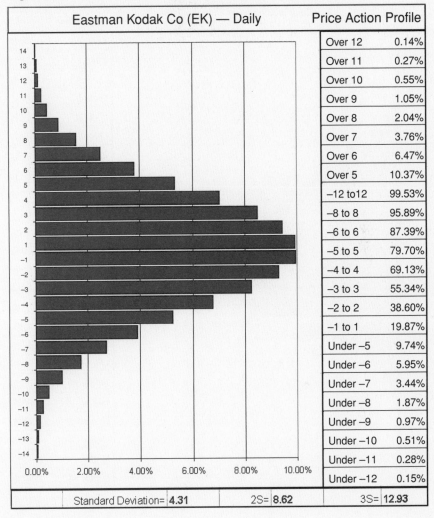

Price Action Profile	
Over 12	0.14%
Over 11	0.27%
Over 10	0.55%
Over 9	1.05%
Over 8	2.04%
Over 7	3.76%
Over 6	6.47%
Over 5	10.37%
−12 to12	99.53%
−8 to 8	95.89%
−6 to 6	87.39%
−5 to 5	79.70%
−4 to 4	69.13%
−3 to 3	55.34%
−2 to 2	38.60%
−1 to 1	19.87%
Under −5	9.74%
Under −6	5.95%
Under −7	3.44%
Under −8	1.87%
Under −9	0.97%
Under −10	0.51%
Under −11	0.28%
Under −12	0.15%

Standard Deviation= **4.31**   2S= **8.62**   3S= **12.93**

Figure A.11 EXXON MOBIL CP (XOM)—Daily Price Action Profile

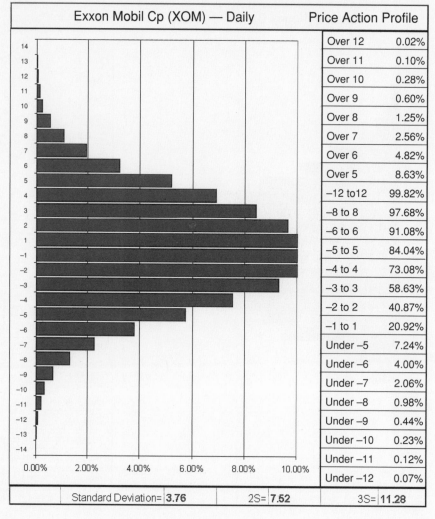

Exxon Mobil Cp (XOM) — Daily	Price Action Profile	
	Over 12	0.02%
	Over 11	0.10%
	Over 10	0.28%
	Over 9	0.60%
	Over 8	1.25%
	Over 7	2.56%
	Over 6	4.82%
	Over 5	8.63%
	−12 to12	99.82%
	−8 to 8	97.68%
	−6 to 6	91.08%
	−5 to 5	84.04%
	−4 to 4	73.08%
	−3 to 3	58.63%
	−2 to 2	40.87%
	−1 to 1	20.92%
	Under −5	7.24%
	Under −6	4.00%
	Under −7	2.06%
	Under −8	0.98%
	Under −9	0.44%
	Under −10	0.23%
	Under −11	0.12%
	Under −12	0.07%

| Standard Deviation= 3.76 | 2S= 7.52 | 3S= 11.28 |

Figure A.12 GENERAL ELECTRIC CO (GE)—Daily Price Action Profile

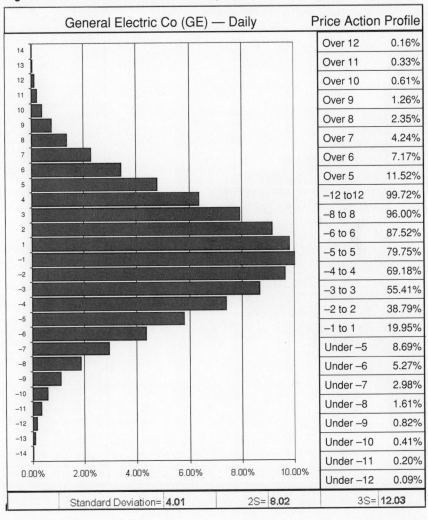

General Electric Co (GE) — Daily	Price Action Profile	
	Over 12	0.16%
	Over 11	0.33%
	Over 10	0.61%
	Over 9	1.26%
	Over 8	2.35%
	Over 7	4.24%
	Over 6	7.17%
	Over 5	11.52%
	−12 to12	99.72%
	−8 to 8	96.00%
	−6 to 6	87.52%
	−5 to 5	79.75%
	−4 to 4	69.18%
	−3 to 3	55.41%
	−2 to 2	38.79%
	−1 to 1	19.95%
	Under −5	8.69%
	Under −6	5.27%
	Under −7	2.98%
	Under −8	1.61%
	Under −9	0.82%
	Under −10	0.41%
	Under −11	0.20%
	Under −12	0.09%

| Standard Deviation= **4.01** | 2S= **8.02** | 3S= **12.03** |

Figure A.13 GENERAL MOTORS CP (GM)—Daily Price Action Profile

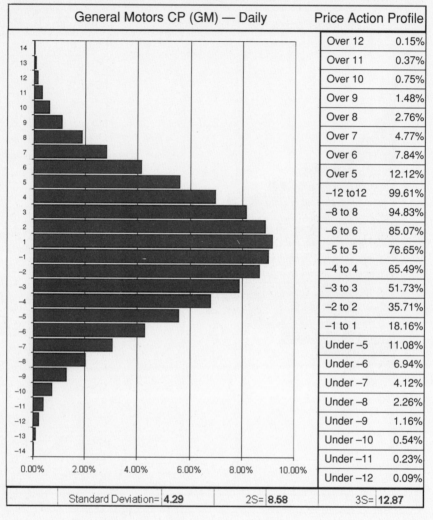

General Motors CP (GM) — Daily	Price Action Profile	
	Over 12	0.15%
	Over 11	0.37%
	Over 10	0.75%
	Over 9	1.48%
	Over 8	2.76%
	Over 7	4.77%
	Over 6	7.84%
	Over 5	12.12%
	−12 to12	99.61%
	−8 to 8	94.83%
	−6 to 6	85.07%
	−5 to 5	76.65%
	−4 to 4	65.49%
	−3 to 3	51.73%
	−2 to 2	35.71%
	−1 to 1	18.16%
	Under −5	11.08%
	Under −6	6.94%
	Under −7	4.12%
	Under −8	2.26%
	Under −9	1.16%
	Under −10	0.54%
	Under −11	0.23%
	Under −12	0.09%
Standard Deviation= **4.29**	2S= **8.58**	3S= **12.87**

Figure A.14   HEWLETT-PACKARD CO (HWP)—Daily Price Action Profile

Hewlett-Packard Co (HWP) — Daily   Price Action Profile

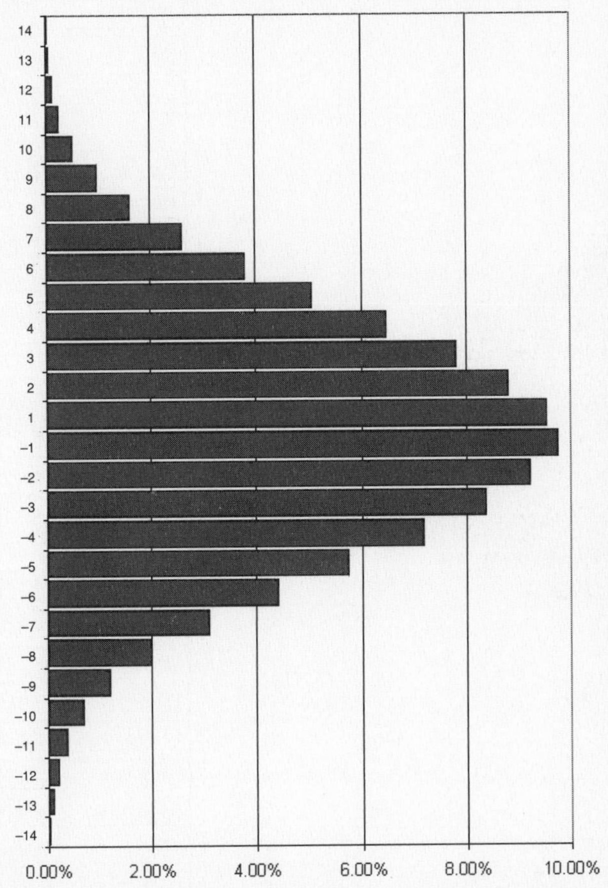

Price Action Profile	
Over 12	0.15%
Over 11	0.33%
Over 10	0.70%
Over 9	1.37%
Over 8	2.56%
Over 7	4.55%
Over 6	7.64%
Over 5	12.03%
−12 to12	99.68%
−8 to 8	95.43%
−6 to 6	86.16%
−5 to 5	77.96%
−4 to 4	67.15%
−3 to 3	53.49%
−2 to 2	37.31%
−1 to 1	19.28%
Under −5	9.94%
Under −6	6.14%
Under −7	3.54%
Under −8	1.94%
Under −9	0.97%
Under −10	0.47%
Under −11	0.22%
Under −12	0.11%

Standard Deviation= **4.20**   2S= **8.40**   3S= **12.60**

Figure A.15   HOME DEPOT INC (HD)—Daily Price Action Profile

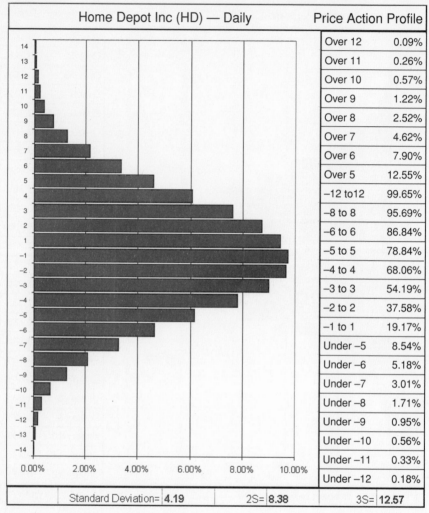

	Price Action Profile
Over 12	0.09%
Over 11	0.26%
Over 10	0.57%
Over 9	1.22%
Over 8	2.52%
Over 7	4.62%
Over 6	7.90%
Over 5	12.55%
−12 to 12	99.65%
−8 to 8	95.69%
−6 to 6	86.84%
−5 to 5	78.84%
−4 to 4	68.06%
−3 to 3	54.19%
−2 to 2	37.58%
−1 to 1	19.17%
Under −5	8.54%
Under −6	5.18%
Under −7	3.01%
Under −8	1.71%
Under −9	0.95%
Under −10	0.56%
Under −11	0.33%
Under −12	0.18%

Standard Deviation= **4.19**   2S= **8.38**   3S= **12.57**

Figure A.16 HONEYWELL INTL (HON)—Daily Price Action Profile

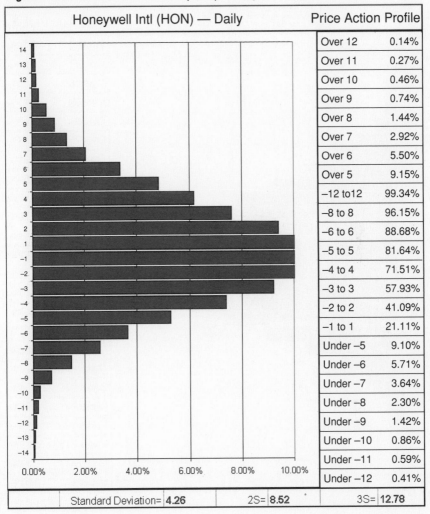

Honeywell Intl (HON) — Daily	Price Action Profile	
	Over 12	0.14%
	Over 11	0.27%
	Over 10	0.46%
	Over 9	0.74%
	Over 8	1.44%
	Over 7	2.92%
	Over 6	5.50%
	Over 5	9.15%
	−12 to12	99.34%
	−8 to 8	96.15%
	−6 to 6	88.68%
	−5 to 5	81.64%
	−4 to 4	71.51%
	−3 to 3	57.93%
	−2 to 2	41.09%
	−1 to 1	21.11%
	Under −5	9.10%
	Under −6	5.71%
	Under −7	3.64%
	Under −8	2.30%
	Under −9	1.42%
	Under −10	0.86%
	Under −11	0.59%
	Under −12	0.41%
Standard Deviation= **4.26**	2S= **8.52**	3S= **12.78**

Figure A.17   INTEL CP (INTC)—Daily Price Action Profile

Intel Cp (INTC) — Daily	Price Action Profile	

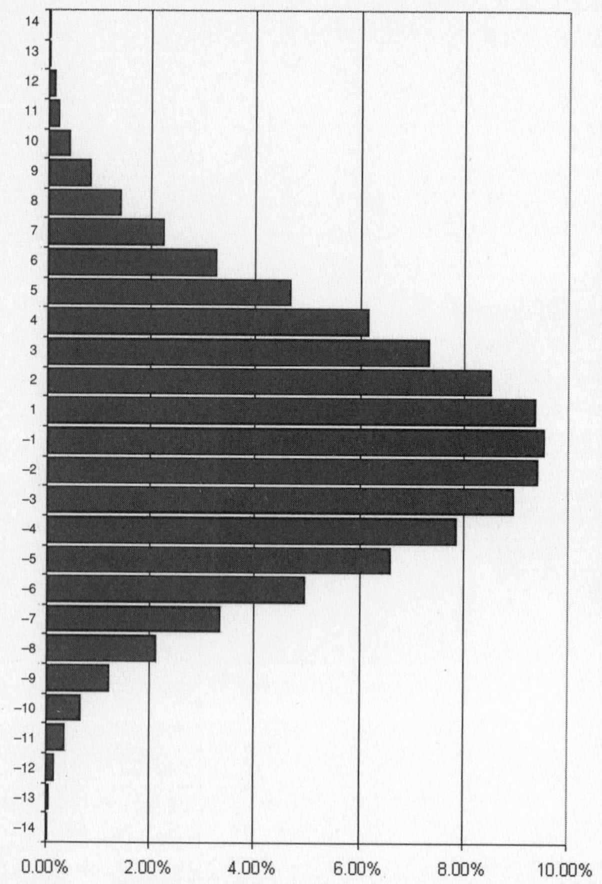

Price Action Profile	
Over 12	0.10%
Over 11	0.24%
Over 10	0.58%
Over 9	1.22%
Over 8	2.45%
Over 7	4.56%
Over 6	7.91%
Over 5	12.88%
−12 to12	99.66%
−8 to 8	95.75%
−6 to 6	86.64%
−5 to 5	78.42%
−4 to 4	67.16%
−3 to 3	53.13%
−2 to 2	36.84%
−1 to 1	18.91%
Under −5	8.52%
Under −6	5.27%
Under −7	3.04%
Under −8	1.63%
Under −9	0.79%
Under −10	0.39%
Under −11	0.18%
Under −12	0.07%

Standard Deviation= 4.02	2S= 8.04	3S= 12.06

Figure A.18 INTL BUSINESS MACHINES (IBM)—Daily Price Action Profile

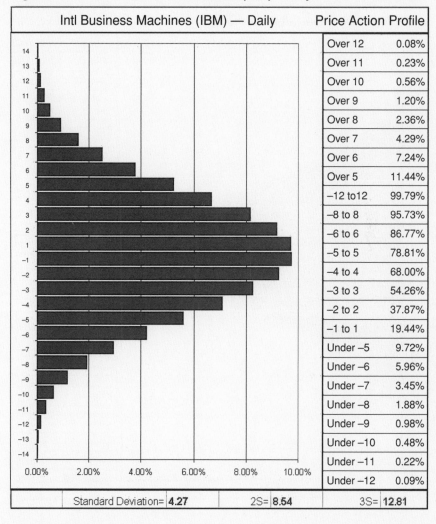

Intl Business Machines (IBM) — Daily	Price Action Profile	
	Over 12	0.08%
	Over 11	0.23%
	Over 10	0.56%
	Over 9	1.20%
	Over 8	2.36%
	Over 7	4.29%
	Over 6	7.24%
	Over 5	11.44%
	−12 to12	99.79%
	−8 to 8	95.73%
	−6 to 6	86.77%
	−5 to 5	78.81%
	−4 to 4	68.00%
	−3 to 3	54.26%
	−2 to 2	37.87%
	−1 to 1	19.44%
	Under −5	9.72%
	Under −6	5.96%
	Under −7	3.45%
	Under −8	1.88%
	Under −9	0.98%
	Under −10	0.48%
	Under −11	0.22%
	Under −12	0.09%
Standard Deviation= **4.27**	2S= **8.54**	3S= **12.81**

Figure A.19 INTL PAPER CO (IP)—Daily Price Action Profile

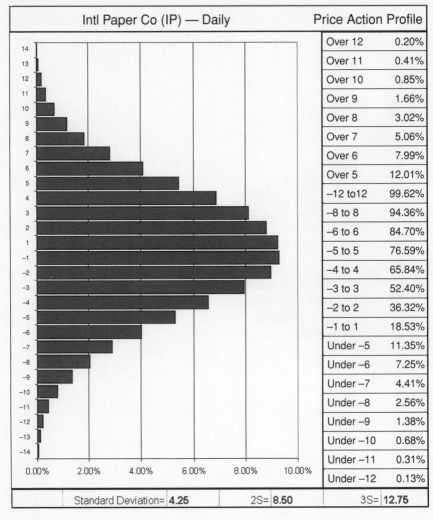

Intl Paper Co (IP) — Daily	Price Action Profile	
	Over 12	0.20%
	Over 11	0.41%
	Over 10	0.85%
	Over 9	1.66%
	Over 8	3.02%
	Over 7	5.06%
	Over 6	7.99%
	Over 5	12.01%
	−12 to12	99.62%
	−8 to 8	94.36%
	−6 to 6	84.70%
	−5 to 5	76.59%
	−4 to 4	65.84%
	−3 to 3	52.40%
	−2 to 2	36.32%
	−1 to 1	18.53%
	Under −5	11.35%
	Under −6	7.25%
	Under −7	4.41%
	Under −8	2.56%
	Under −9	1.38%
	Under −10	0.68%
	Under −11	0.31%
	Under −12	0.13%
Standard Deviation= **4.25**	2S= **8.50**	3S= **12.75**

Figure A.20 JP MORGAN CHASE & CO (JPM)—Daily Price Action Profile

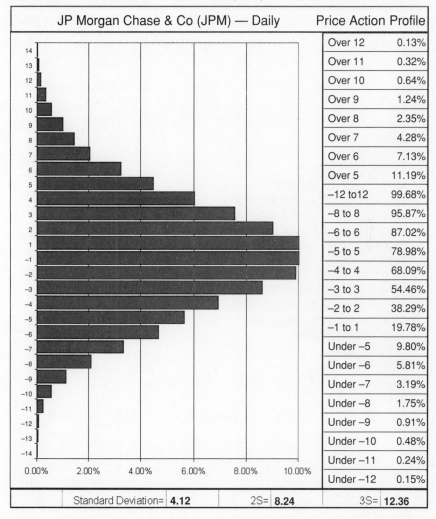

JP Morgan Chase & Co (JPM) — Daily	Price Action Profile	
	Over 12	0.13%
	Over 11	0.32%
	Over 10	0.64%
	Over 9	1.24%
	Over 8	2.35%
	Over 7	4.28%
	Over 6	7.13%
	Over 5	11.19%
	−12 to12	99.68%
	−8 to 8	95.87%
	−6 to 6	87.02%
	−5 to 5	78.98%
	−4 to 4	68.09%
	−3 to 3	54.46%
	−2 to 2	38.29%
	−1 to 1	19.78%
	Under −5	9.80%
	Under −6	5.81%
	Under −7	3.19%
	Under −8	1.75%
	Under −9	0.91%
	Under −10	0.48%
	Under −11	0.24%
	Under −12	0.15%
Standard Deviation= **4.12**	2S= **8.24**	3S= **12.36**

Figure A.21   JOHNSON & JOHNSON (JNJ)—Daily Price Action Profile

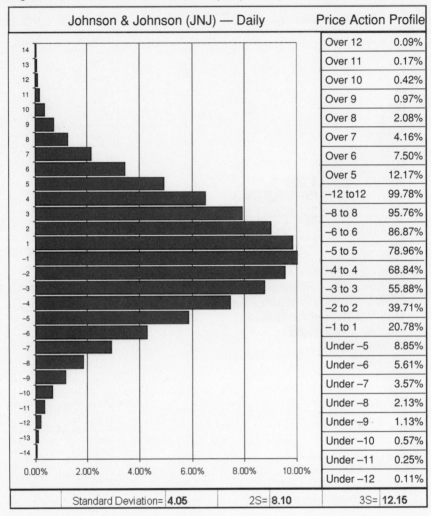

Johnson & Johnson (JNJ) — Daily	Price Action Profile	
	Over 12	0.09%
	Over 11	0.17%
	Over 10	0.42%
	Over 9	0.97%
	Over 8	2.08%
	Over 7	4.16%
	Over 6	7.50%
	Over 5	12.17%
	−12 to12	99.78%
	−8 to 8	95.76%
	−6 to 6	86.87%
	−5 to 5	78.96%
	−4 to 4	68.84%
	−3 to 3	55.88%
	−2 to 2	39.71%
	−1 to 1	20.78%
	Under −5	8.85%
	Under −6	5.61%
	Under −7	3.57%
	Under −8	2.13%
	Under −9	1.13%
	Under −10	0.57%
	Under −11	0.25%
	Under −12	0.11%

| Standard Deviation= **4.05** | 2S= **8.10** | 3S= **12.15** |

Figure A.22 MCDONALD'S CP (MCD)—Daily Price Action Profile

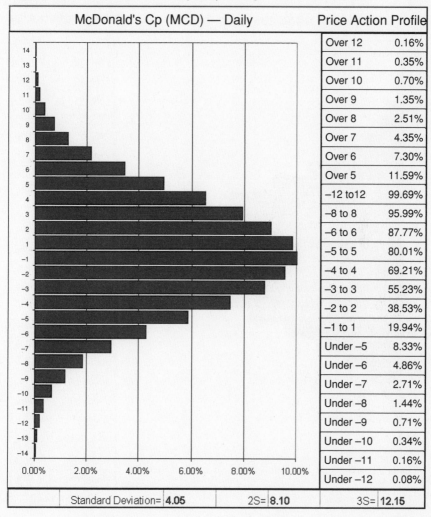

McDonald's Cp (MCD) — Daily	Price Action Profile	
	Over 12	0.16%
	Over 11	0.35%
	Over 10	0.70%
	Over 9	1.35%
	Over 8	2.51%
	Over 7	4.35%
	Over 6	7.30%
	Over 5	11.59%
	−12 to12	99.69%
	−8 to 8	95.99%
	−6 to 6	87.77%
	−5 to 5	80.01%
	−4 to 4	69.21%
	−3 to 3	55.23%
	−2 to 2	38.53%
	−1 to 1	19.94%
	Under −5	8.33%
	Under −6	4.86%
	Under −7	2.71%
	Under −8	1.44%
	Under −9	0.71%
	Under −10	0.34%
	Under −11	0.16%
	Under −12	0.08%
Standard Deviation= **4.05**	2S= **8.10**	3S= **12.15**

Figure A.23 MERCK & CO INC (MRK)—Daily Price Action Profile

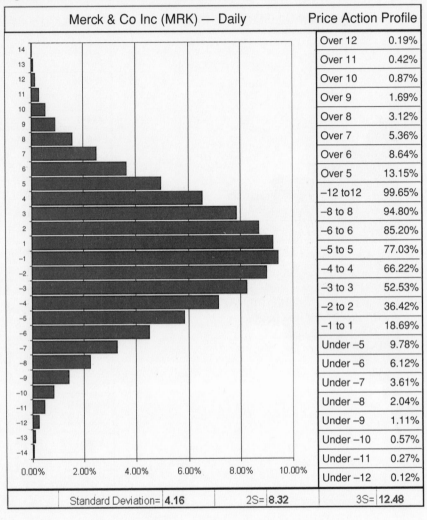

Merck & Co Inc (MRK) — Daily	Price Action Profile	
	Over 12	0.19%
	Over 11	0.42%
	Over 10	0.87%
	Over 9	1.69%
	Over 8	3.12%
	Over 7	5.36%
	Over 6	8.64%
	Over 5	13.15%
	−12 to12	99.65%
	−8 to 8	94.80%
	−6 to 6	85.20%
	−5 to 5	77.03%
	−4 to 4	66.22%
	−3 to 3	52.53%
	−2 to 2	36.42%
	−1 to 1	18.69%
	Under −5	9.78%
	Under −6	6.12%
	Under −7	3.61%
	Under −8	2.04%
	Under −9	1.11%
	Under −10	0.57%
	Under −11	0.27%
	Under −12	0.12%
Standard Deviation= **4.16**	2S= **8.32**	3S= **12.48**

Figure A.24 MICROSOFT CP (MSFT)—Daily Price Action Profile

Microsoft Cp (MSFT) — Daily	Price Action Profile	
	Over 12	0.14%
	Over 11	0.31%
	Over 10	0.62%
	Over 9	1.21%
	Over 8	2.23%
	Over 7	4.03%
	Over 6	7.02%
	Over 5	11.37%
	−12 to12	99.77%
	−8 to 8	96.20%
	−6 to 6	88.12%
	−5 to 5	80.55%
	−4 to 4	69.84%
	−3 to 3	56.12%
	−2 to 2	39.36%
	−1 to 1	20.27%
	Under −5	8.06%
	Under −6	4.84%
	Under −7	2.72%
	Under −8	1.54%
	Under −9	0.73%
	Under −10	0.28%
	Under −11	0.12%
	Under −12	0.06%

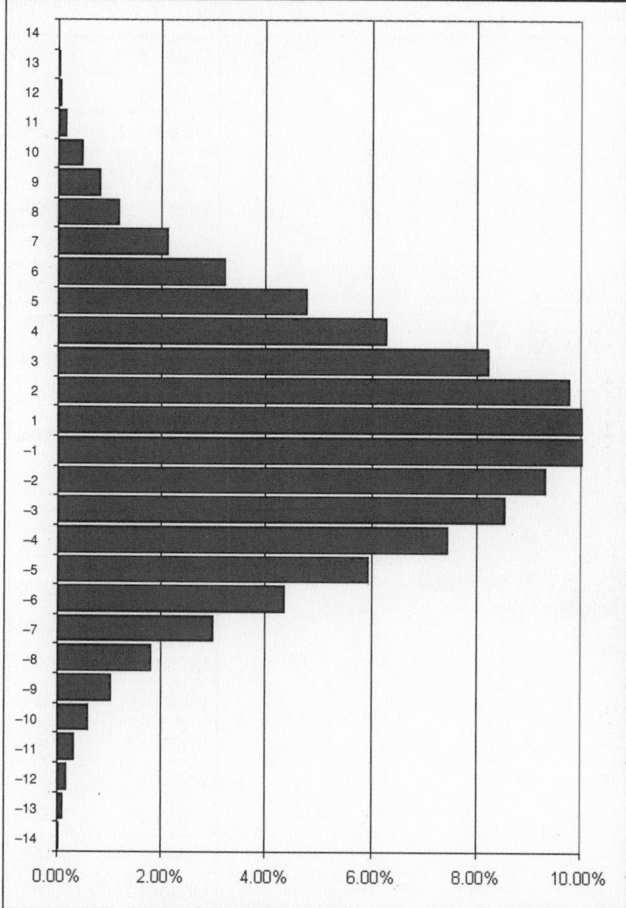

Standard Deviation= 4.08   2S= 8.16   3S= 12.24

Figure A.25 MINNESOTA MINING & MFG CO (MMM)—Daily Price Action Profile

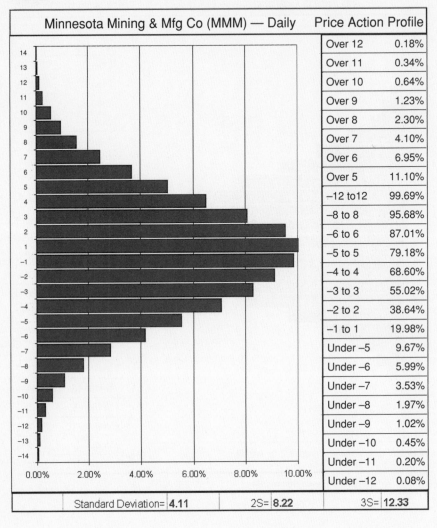

Minnesota Mining & Mfg Co (MMM) — Daily	Price Action Profile	
	Over 12	0.18%
	Over 11	0.34%
	Over 10	0.64%
	Over 9	1.23%
	Over 8	2.30%
	Over 7	4.10%
	Over 6	6.95%
	Over 5	11.10%
	−12 to12	99.69%
	−8 to 8	95.68%
	−6 to 6	87.01%
	−5 to 5	79.18%
	−4 to 4	68.60%
	−3 to 3	55.02%
	−2 to 2	38.64%
	−1 to 1	19.98%
	Under −5	9.67%
	Under −6	5.99%
	Under −7	3.53%
	Under −8	1.97%
	Under −9	1.02%
	Under −10	0.45%
	Under −11	0.20%
	Under −12	0.08%
Standard Deviation= **4.11**	2S= **8.22**	3S= **12.33**

Figure A.26 PHILIP MORRIS COS INC (MO)—Daily Price Action Profile

Philip Morris Cos Inc (MO) — Daily	Price Action Profile	
	Over 12	0.22%
	Over 11	0.43%
	Over 10	0.87%
	Over 9	1.65%
	Over 8	2.97%
	Over 7	5.17%
	Over 6	8.43%
	Over 5	12.97%
	−12 to 12	99.53%
	−8 to 8	94.92%
	−6 to 6	85.69%
	−5 to 5	77.71%
	−4 to 4	66.94%
	−3 to 3	53.33%
	−2 to 2	37.03%
	−1 to 1	18.93%
	Under −5	9.19%
	Under −6	5.74%
	Under −7	3.45%
	Under −8	1.98%
	Under −9	1.06%
	Under −10	0.54%
	Under −11	0.26%
	Under −12	0.12%
Standard Deviation= 4.28	2S= 8.56	3S= 12.84

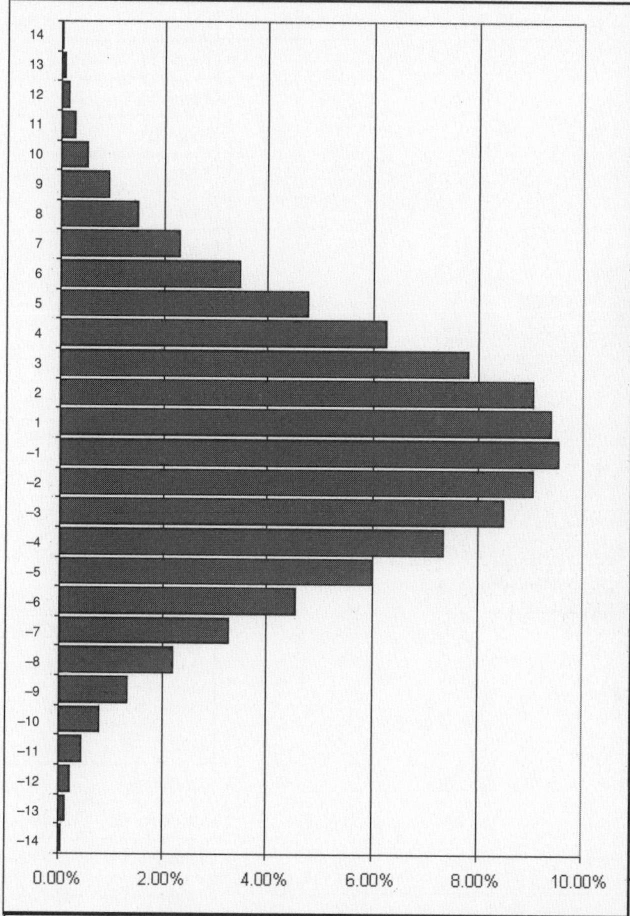

Figure A.27 PROCTER & GAMBLE CO (PG)—Daily Price Action Profile

Procter & Gamble Co (PG) — Daily	Price Action Profile	
	Over 12	0.12%
	Over 11	0.28%
	Over 10	0.61%
	Over 9	1.25%
	Over 8	2.36%
	Over 7	4.23%
	Over 6	7.15%
	Over 5	11.46%
	−12 to 12	99.77%
	−8 to 8	95.85%
	−6 to 6	87.19%
	−5 to 5	79.14%
	−4 to 4	68.18%
	−3 to 3	54.56%
	−2 to 2	38.05%
	−1 to 1	19.55%
	Under −5	9.38%
	Under −6	5.65%
	Under −7	3.20%
	Under −8	1.78%
	Under −9	0.93%
	Under −10	0.45%
	Under −11	0.22%
	Under −12	0.10%
Standard Deviation= **3.84**	2S= **7.68**	3S= **11.52**

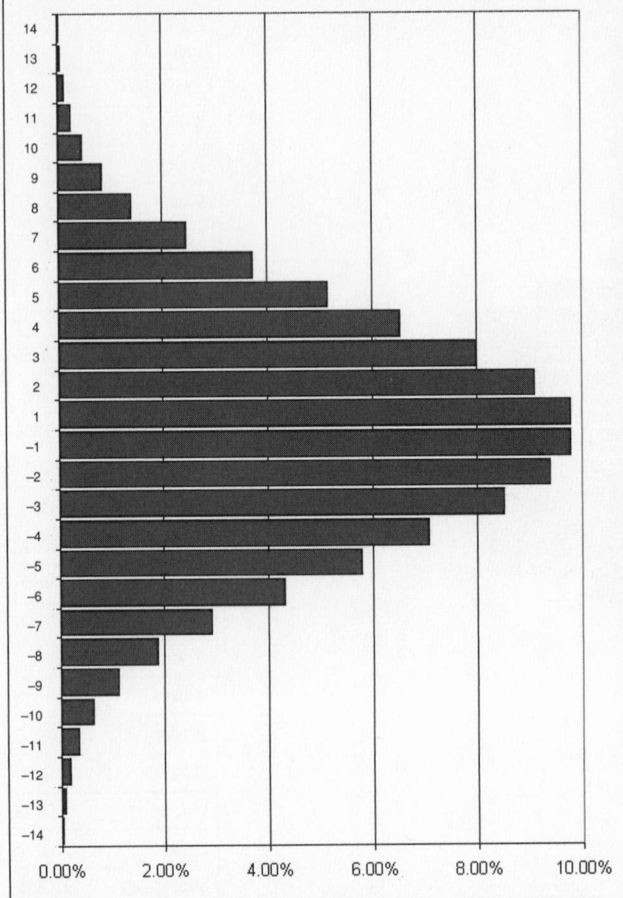

Figure A.28 SBC COMMUNICATION (SBC)—Daily Price Action Profile

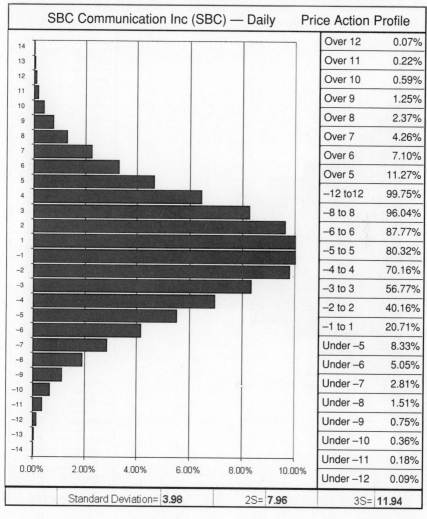

SBC Communication Inc (SBC) — Daily	Price Action Profile	
	Over 12	0.07%
	Over 11	0.22%
	Over 10	0.59%
	Over 9	1.25%
	Over 8	2.37%
	Over 7	4.26%
	Over 6	7.10%
	Over 5	11.27%
	−12 to12	99.75%
	−8 to 8	96.04%
	−6 to 6	87.77%
	−5 to 5	80.32%
	−4 to 4	70.16%
	−3 to 3	56.77%
	−2 to 2	40.16%
	−1 to 1	20.71%
	Under −5	8.33%
	Under −6	5.05%
	Under −7	2.81%
	Under −8	1.51%
	Under −9	0.75%
	Under −10	0.36%
	Under −11	0.18%
	Under −12	0.09%
Standard Deviation= **3.98**	2S= **7.96**	3S= **11.94**

Figure A.29 UNITED TECHNOLOGIES CP (UTX)—Daily Price Action Profile

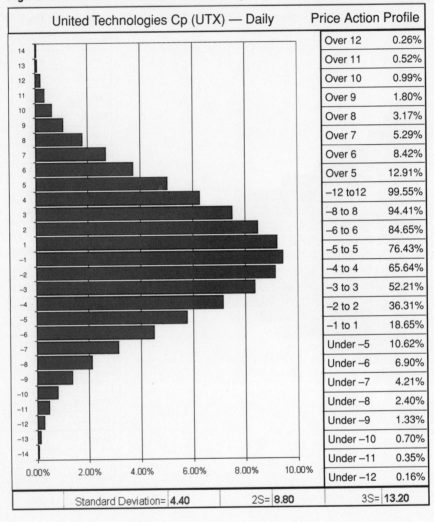

United Technologies Cp (UTX) — Daily	Price Action Profile	
	Over 12	0.26%
	Over 11	0.52%
	Over 10	0.99%
	Over 9	1.80%
	Over 8	3.17%
	Over 7	5.29%
	Over 6	8.42%
	Over 5	12.91%
	−12 to12	99.55%
	−8 to 8	94.41%
	−6 to 6	84.65%
	−5 to 5	76.43%
	−4 to 4	65.64%
	−3 to 3	52.21%
	−2 to 2	36.31%
	−1 to 1	18.65%
	Under −5	10.62%
	Under −6	6.90%
	Under −7	4.21%
	Under −8	2.40%
	Under −9	1.33%
	Under −10	0.70%
	Under −11	0.35%
	Under −12	0.16%
Standard Deviation= 4.40	2S= 8.80	3S= 13.20

Figure A.30 WAL-MART STORES INC (WMT)—Daily Price Action Profile

Wal-Mart Stores Inc (WMT) — Daily	Price Action Profile	
	Over 12	0.02%
	Over 11	0.10%
	Over 10	0.29%
	Over 9	0.80%
	Over 8	1.82%
	Over 7	3.51%
	Over 6	6.54%
	Over 5	11.28%
	−12 to12	99.83%
	−8 to 8	96.90%
	−6 to 6	88.79%
	−5 to 5	80.80%
	−4 to 4	69.85%
	−3 to 3	56.23%
	−2 to 2	39.51%
	−1 to 1	20.16%
	Under −5	7.84%
	Under −6	4.59%
	Under −7	2.40%
	Under −8	1.20%
	Under −9	0.56%
	Under −10	0.25%
	Under −11	0.12%
	Under −12	0.07%
Standard Deviation= **3.94**	2S= **7.88**	3S= **11.82**

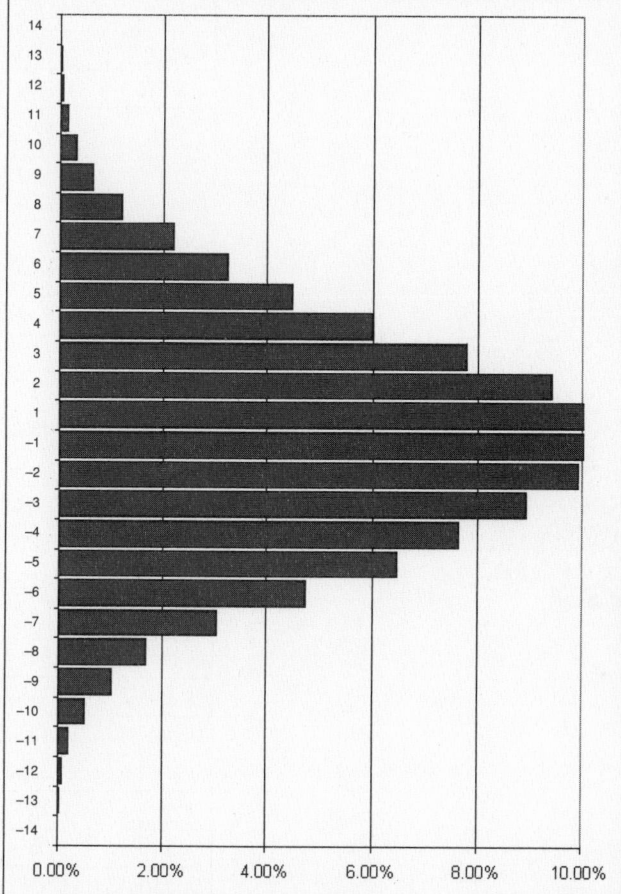

Index